Advance Praise for *The Temple at the End of the Universe*

"A gorgeously written and immaculately considered interrogation into faith in the age of climate change. Simultaneously demanding and stirring, *The Temple at the End of the Universe* is a necessary companion for anyone questing for meaning under dark-looming clouds while questioning their place in the future of the world. This is a book that speaks to the imperilled soul of our moment."

— Harley Rustad, bestselling author of
Lost in the Valley of Death and *Big Lonely Doug*

"Josiah Neufeld's fascinating quest is both a memoir and investigation into religion's attempts — and refusals — to confront the ecological crisis facing modern society and the natural world. This is an urgent and beautifully written exploration of the search for a new understanding."

— Deborah Campbell, Hilary Weston Prize–winning author of
A Disappearance in Damascus

"A fascinating journey, described in clear and compelling prose, from stifling certainty to constructive questioning. Anyone who's tried to make sense of the deformed Christianity that wields so much power in our world will profit from this book — and so will anyone who's on a quest of their own, determined to figure out how to help this beautiful and ailing planet."

— Bill McKibben, author of
The Flag, the Cross, and the Station Wagon

"A spiritual quest has a whole new meaning when the natural world as we know it is in peril, and we could not ask for a better companion on the journey than Josiah Neufeld. His curiosity, insight, and honesty in *The Temple at the End of the Universe* are extraordinary."

— Joan Thomas, Governor General Award–winning author of
Five Wives

THE
TEMPLE
AT THE END
OF THE
UNIVERSE

A SEARCH FOR SPIRITUALITY
IN THE ANTHROPOCENE

JOSIAH NEUFELD

ANANSI

Published in Canada in 2023 and the USA in 2023 by House of Anansi Press Inc.
houseofanansi.com

House of Anansi Press is committed to protecting our natural environment. This book is made of material from well-managed FSC®-certified forests, recycled materials, and other controlled sources.

House of Anansi Press is a Global Certified Accessible™ (GCA by Benetech) publisher. The ebook version of this book meets stringent accessibility standards and is available to readers with print disabilities.

27 26 25 24 23   1 2 3 4 5

Library and Archives Canada Cataloguing in Publication

Title: The temple at the end of the universe :
a search for spirituality in the Anthropocene / Josiah Neufeld.
Names: Neufeld, Josiah, author.
Description: Includes bibliographical references.
Identifiers: Canadiana (print) 20230138381 | Canadiana (ebook) 2023013839X |
ISBN 9781487010638 (softcover) | ISBN 9781487010645 (EPUB)
Subjects: LCSH: Neufeld, Josiah—Religion. | LCSH: Ecology—Religious aspects. | LCSH: Climatic changes—Religious aspects. | LCSH: Environmental protection—Religious aspects. | LCSH: Environmental ethics. | LCSH: Ecotheology.
Classification: LCC BL65.E36 N48 2023 | DDC 201/.77—dc23

Book design: Lucia Kim
Cover image: AscentXmedia @ iStock

Every reasonable effort has been made to trace ownership of copyright materials. The publisher will gladly rectify any inadvertent errors or omissions in credits in future editions.

House of Anansi Press is grateful for the privilege to work on and create from the Traditional Territory of many Nations, including the Anishinabeg, the Wendat, and the Haudenosaunee, as well as the Treaty Lands of the Mississaugas of the Credit.

With the participation of the Government of Canada
Avec la participation du gouvernement du Canada

We acknowledge for their financial support of our publishing program the Canada Council for the Arts, the Ontario Arts Council, and the Government of Canada.

Printed and bound in Canada

MIX
Paper from responsible sources
FSC
www.fsc.org   FSC® C103567

For my children

CONTENTS

AUTHOR'S NOTE

ON MY SIXTEENTH BIRTHDAY my long-haired, philosophical, truck-driving uncle gave me a book. I still have it. The pages are yellowed; the dust jacket's sparkling constellations and planetary diagrams have been torn and Scotch-taped. It's *The Hitchhiker's Guide to the Galaxy*, Douglas Adams's hilarious and irreverent five-part "trilogy" centred around the hapless Arthur Dent, whose planet (Earth) is demolished to make way for an interplanetary bypass, and his quest to find the answer to "life, the universe and everything." The second of the five books contained in the omnibus volume is called *The Restaurant at the End of the Universe* and features a restaurant built on a ruined planet and enclosed in a time bubble from which one can watch the universe end while enjoying an elaborate breakfast. At the time I received the book, I was a committed evangelical Christian who had made several wholly unsuccessful attempts to convert my agnostic uncle back to Christianity and rescue his imperilled soul. I loved him dearly, so this was important. But my uncle preferred absurdity to piety, and *The Hitchhiker's Guide* was something of a sacred text for him. The book made me laugh so hard I was able to ignore how profane it was, which was probably the whole idea.

This anecdote might seem like a strange point of reference for a book about how religious and spiritual communities are grappling with the ecological peril facing our species and many others, a deeply earnest inquiry if ever there was one. But sometimes we need a little absurdity to shake up our earnestness and stir our imagination. I believe a significant shift in human consciousness is underway. Theology has much in common with science fiction: despite their otherworldly reputations, both, in essence, imagine what new worlds are possible within the world we presently inhabit. So it feels oddly appropriate here to salute the spirit of Douglas Adams, wherever he is, probably thumbing a ride across the infinite cosmos, and thank him for a book that interrupted the serious convictions of my childhood and helped nudge me along on my own search for answers to life, the universe, and everything.

I grew up believing in a God who had ordered the universe and was firmly in charge of its fate. At some point in my early adulthood I began to question that cosmology. I put down the guidebook I'd been given and began to explore other scriptures, both sacred and secular. This book you are holding is, in many ways, an argument between the believer in my heart and the skeptic in my head. A friend once told me she has both a believer and an unbeliever living inside her. That image stayed with me. Both characters live in me too: the doubter and the devotee, the journalist and the poet, the ego and the soul.

This book contains plenty of skeptics, people who asked dangerous questions at critical moments. It is also full of believers, people who fervently pursued their visions for a more just world. And it contains a third category: mystics, those who wander the fringes of belief consumed by spiritual thirst, often gifted with another sight. Skeptics, believers, and mystics have all been my guides and teachers. I hope some of them will be yours as well. So don't panic. The times we live in are not easy, but there are many worthy companions along the way.

Chapter 1

LOST

A WORD OF WARNING: This book is for those who are lost. If you are already found, put it down. If you hope this book will lead you to spiritual truth, I am sorry in advance. If you already possess the answers, this book is not for you. This book will not confirm what you already know. It will only lead you deeper into mystery, into thirst, into wonder. The spiritual guides I have turned to in the writing of it — Etty Hillesum, Jesus of Nazareth, Mary Oliver — are not people who found their way. They are people who got lost. Who set themselves adrift. Who wandered. I follow them in their thirst because I too want to burn with the fire of their quest. I follow them not because they have found something but because they have searched for it with devotion.

Read on if you are prepared to glimpse the promised land from a distance but never set foot in it. I cannot lead you to truth, but I can lead you on a strange and wondrous road. Come with me if you can. If you have no choice.

I STARTED WRITING THIS book during a global lockdown in 2020, as a plague began its rampage across the
world and so many of us watched it unfold from our
bedroom offices. I can tell you that there is no worse time
to begin writing a nonfiction book. For a week I sat at my
desk and stared at spring sunlight coming through window-
panes filmed by a winter of grime. I stared at the greys and
browns and yellows of early spring: dead leaves, winter-
seared grass, skeletal trees waiting for new buds. I scrolled
through the daily statistics and watched the steep upward
climb of deaths and tried to imagine the shape of the book
in front of me. I had already spent a year reading books,
reporting, interviewing activists and priests and scientists
and theologians. I was trying to map out a book about one
planetary crisis while staring another one in the face. The
council of questions I had collected seemed untrustworthy
in the strange light of this new reality in which human
touch and physical solidarity was forbidden. Which of
my questions still mattered in this new world? Everything
I had imagined about the apocalypse seemed insubstantial
in light of an actual one. And yet the question I was wres-
tling with — How do you write a book for a world you
never imagined? — was exactly the question I had set out
to address long before the pandemic appeared. Perhaps
there was no *better* time to start.

One morning, after a week of false starts, I woke up
from a dream that left my mouth cottony with guilt. In my
dream, my young son kept wandering out of his bedroom,
red-eyed and tousled, to complain that he couldn't sleep.

My partner, Mona, and I, trying to enjoy a few moments of peace after another long day locked in a small house with two energetic children, kept telling him to go back to bed.

"Of course you can't fall asleep," I snapped, still in my dream. "You keep getting up."

"But I'm scared of my blanket."

How could his blanket scare him? He'd been sleeping under it since he was three. "There's nothing scary about your blanket. Just go to sleep. I don't want you to come out here again."

"Come see," he insisted.

Angrily, I got up and propelled him back to his bedroom. When I entered his room, I saw what he meant. His blanket was covered with tiny houses. A metropolis had sprung up on the fabric, like mushrooms on a damp forest floor. Each window burned with a weird interior light. I snatched the haunted blanket off the bed and carried it out of the room. Under the frank glare of the light bulb in the hallway, the blanket was ordinary again, covered, as always, with cartoon rabbits. I threw it into the guest room and found my son another blanket for the night. I woke from the dream feeling sweaty, confused, and contrite.

Dreams leave behind an emotional residue that can colour a day or a week. This one left me coated in self-reproach. I knew I needed more patience. But when I examined my feelings, I realized I was upset, not so much because I'd responded harshly to my worried son but because in my dream I'd had no explanation to offer him for the strange phenomenon we had witnessed. Despite everything I knew about the nature of reality, his irrational fears had proven valid. I was faced with the fact that I did not know the way forward. I had no coherent story that explained the world. Having set aside the narrative that sheltered me as a child, I had none to give my children. I had no story that would guide them through the nightmares that I feared would attend their lives. My young daughter had begun to play imaginative games that opened with some variation of "My parents both died. Can I live with you?"

I didn't know what to do.

We need a new story, wrote the late Catholic priest and eco-theologian Thomas Berry. The old story, the biblical one about the creation of the world and the place of humans within it, had sustained us for a long time. It had taught us the meaning of suffering, explained the origins of evil, provided us with purpose, and showed us how to live. In the old story, the primordial human fault was being steadily repaired as human history moved toward its ultimate fulfillment. But the old story was no longer working, Berry said. The old story did not have room for scientific understandings of the fourteen-billion-year history of our galaxy or the emergence of human consciousness — the moment the universe became aware of itself. A purely secular scientific understanding of the world wasn't adequate either. It couldn't provide us with sufficient meaning or the social discipline necessary to lead spiritually fulfilled lives. We needed a story that was both scientific and spiritual, Berry said, a story that could provide morality, meaning, healing, and guidance in an age of ecological crisis. A story with liturgies to celebrate the formation of our solar system and the miracle of photosynthesis and rituals to lament the species we were driving to extinction, each one a unique expression of divine presence. A story that could teach humans about the evolution of life and the mystery of existence and our place as part of an interdependent whole. We would either learn our proper place on the earth or we would destroy it.

I GREW UP IN the bosom of Christianity. When I was three, my parents, evangelical Mennonites from southern Manitoba, travelled across the world to Burkina Faso, where they settled in a tiny village of Muslims whom they hoped to convert to Christianity. They brought with them the Bible and *Where There Is No Doctor*, books full of apocalyptic scenes, grotesque maladies, and DIY remedies for body and soul.

My earliest intimations of the apocalypse came from reading an article, possibly in *National Geographic*, about the inexorable advance of the Sahara Desert. I remember lying in bed worrying, imagining a future without water. Although the village where we lived was lush and green in rainy season, dry season brought a haze of fine white desert dust that settled in every crevice of clothing and skin and turned the setting sun into a blood-red ball. I knew from reading the Bible that the world would one day be destroyed and God would sit on his throne and sort the sheep from the goats. The sheep, a small minority, would go with God into eternal bliss, while everyone else, including the boys with whom I hunted lizards and played soccer, would be tossed into a lake of fire.

My friend Mamadou, like everyone else in the village, grew the food his family lived on. He tried to teach me to cultivate with his wide-bladed hoe. My furrows meandered, my hands blistered, and my delicate white skin burned in the sun. I taught him to play UNO, riffle-shuffling the deck with a dexterity that made him shake his head. I prayed for Mamadou nightly.

By the standards of middle-class Canadians, my family was poor: our toilet was an outhouse and we pulled our drinking water from a well. But next to our neighbours in the village, we were millionaires. Children pressed their noses against the screen door of our porch and marvelled at the wonders our house contained. Solar panels on our roof powered electric lights, fans, radios, and my dad's Toshiba laptop with its mysterious green screen and blinking cursor. We had rooms full of books. We owned the only vehicle in the village, a Peugeot pickup truck, which frequently served as the village ambulance. Mamadou and my other friends constantly asked me for things — Band-Aids, flashlight batteries, pens. I longed to bridge the social and economic abyss between us, but the constant requests nettled me. I could never be sure if they were my friends because they liked me or because they wanted what I had. My awareness of this class divide was sharpened by an unspoken competition among the other missionaries to see who could live most like the locals. If we wanted our neighbours to listen to the good news, the missionary logic went, we would have to live like them. One family built a cluster of one-room mud-brick houses that put our sprawling cinder-block house with its peaked tin roof and colonial porch to shame.

Of course, try as we might to live in true solidarity with our neighbours, it was an impossible bar. Even the most righteously poor among the missionaries still sent their children to boarding school and made emergency trips to a sterile hospital run by American Baptists and flew across the ocean to visit family.

On furlough in Canada, my siblings and I marvelled at cold bricks of cheddar cheese and orderly rivers of cars and electric toasters and carpeted basements. The homes of the generous church people we visited were crammed with things that surely no one in human history had ever needed before: electric shavers, microwave ovens, furry toilet seat covers.

Witnessing these disparities taught me that the world was fundamentally unjust and nothing I could do would alter this fact. And layered on top of my worldly privileges was another, unworldly one. After a life of comfort, I would go to heaven; after a life of poverty, my friends would go to hell. I never doubted the inevitability of the apocalypse nor God's willingness to unleash it. But even as a child, I sensed its gross injustice.

That apocalypse never arrived, although American authors Tim LaHaye and Jerry B. Jenkins capitalized on the evangelical fear of it with their sixteen-volume *Left Behind* series, based on the theological premise that Christ will return one day soon to snatch away the faithful few, leaving the unsaved masses to suffer famine, pestilence, and war. The series sold eighty million copies and was made into a film starring Nicolas Cage. I didn't read the books, but the feathery voice of Christian rocker Larry Norman crooning "I Wish We'd All Been Ready" still rings in my ears.

I hung on to some version of this eschatology until a contrarian professor at the Bible college I attended in my early twenties pointed out that in Jesus's story in the Gospel of Matthew foretelling the end of the age — the story Norman's song and the entire *Left Behind* series are ostensibly premised on — the *unrighteous* are taken and the righteous ones are left behind.

Almost two decades later, I sat in a café, nervously stirring a bowl of lukewarm soup, mustering up the courage to tell my mother I no longer believed in God. I believed in something: a presence or a cosmic current of love or the earth itself. But I could tell there wasn't enough overlap between her vocabulary and mine — I was rejecting everything she had dedicated her life to.

"I don't believe in God," I said. "But I still love god."

She stared at me through tears and prodded at her dessert with her fork. "That doesn't make any sense."

I knew it didn't. I tried to describe my notion of a spiritual realm intermeshed with the physical one. "I think love is more important than belief anyway," I said, trailing off. I was sure it all sounded like garbled fluff to her. The café was closing. We stood up and put on our coats.

"What would it take," I asked, "for you to recognize that my spiritual search is as genuine and sincere as yours?" She scrunched her forehead and failed to summon an answer.

FOR ME, THE APOCALYPSE became real in the summer of 2019. That summer I read two alarming books — Elizabeth Kolbert's *The Sixth Extinction* and David Wallace-Wells's *The Uninhabitable Earth* — and learned more than a few terrifying facts. The last of the world's forests, which helped regulate rainfall, sheltered species, and influenced ocean currents, were being weakened by a heating atmosphere and were swiftly falling to chainsaws and fire and hungry invasive insects. One million species of animals and plants were threatened with extinction. Carbon dioxide concentrations in our atmosphere had reached a level not seen since before human civilizations evolved.

That summer, the Amazon burned and Brazilian president Jair Bolsonaro told the Indigenous Peoples fighting for the forest's life to go to hell. A tantrum-prone reality TV show host, unfortunately sitting at the helm of the most powerful country on earth, forged ahead with his plans to withdraw from the Paris Climate Accord. That summer twelve municipalities in my home province of Manitoba declared states of agricultural disaster due to drought, and Prime Minister Justin Trudeau announced a climate emergency one day and approved a massive fossil fuel pipeline expansion the next.

The summer of drought gave way to an autumn of deluge. The City of Winnipeg opened its floodway, something that had never before occurred in the fall. A freak storm dumped enough wet snow on the city to tear the limbs from thirty thousand trees. Greta Thunberg brought her rebuke to North America by boat from Sweden. As people around the world flooded public squares to urge their governments to answer the climate crisis with the emergency measures it required, twelve thousand people massed on the lawn of Winnipeg's legislative buildings. I was among them, wearing a reflective vest and trying to keep the crowds from boiling over from the designated route. My heart was full of hope. Finally the people were rising, and nobody could ignore us. The experience was short-lived. Our premier did not make an appearance, and soon thereafter he cut funding to environmental groups and sued the federal government over its carbon tax. A friend's five-year-old daughter asked her father if the earth would still be alive when she died, and I cried real tears for my children. As I tried to explain to them what was happening, a hollow helplessness formed behind my breastbone. I wondered once again, as I had many times before, if I should turn back to my childhood faith. Now would be a good time for an interventionist God.

IN LATE OCTOBER, I dropped off my children with their grandparents and left on a five-day canoe trip, out of reach of Twitter and the onrush of daily news. I went with my uncle, the one who'd given me *The Hitchhiker's Guide*, and my cousin, a massage therapist with a degree in environmental science, who, like me, seemed to carry the burden of our imperilled planet as a physical weight on her shoulders. We paddled a coiling 70-kilometre stretch of the Manigotagan River between granite humps and reedy wetlands, through forests of jack pine and black spruce and trembling aspen and paper birch. Daytime temperatures hovered a few degrees above freezing, but the sloping autumn sun warmed our shoulders and ignited halos among the last golden leaves on the white-trunked aspens along the shore. The river was swollen and rambunctious after the rainy fall. If anyone tipped, we knew we'd have to stop and build a fire to get warm, so we portaged all but the gentlest rapids. On our first night, we pitched camp on a shoulder of pink-streaked granite, tie-dyed with milky-white rings of lichen. We sat around the fire as dusk drifted into darkness. My cousin and I talked about ecological breakdown.

"We're more likely to see an economic collapse than an environmental one," my uncle said dismissively.

My cousin and I exchanged glances. "It'll be the same thing, when it comes," she said.

My uncle leaned back in his camp chair. "Okay. Sure. Let me play devil's advocate for a minute —"

"I don't even see what's the point of doing that," my cousin interrupted. She started to cry. "I really don't have any interest in making this into an intellectual exercise. I just want to have a future. We're way past the point of *solving* the climate crisis. Now we're just trying to survive. We're fighting with everything we've got." My uncle poked at the fire. I stared into the embers and tried to think of something hopeful to say.

The next few days were crisp and lovely. We knew we were tempting fate by canoeing so late in the season, but the river gods smiled, granting us the only few consecutive days of sunlight in that long and dreary fall. We passed otters and beavers and golden-eye ducks and grey jays and leopard frogs and a pair of young moose up to their shoulders in cattails. Around every bend we startled squadrons of honking swans off the water. We caught and ate a giant pickerel, sautéed with onions and dates.

One evening my cousin and I stayed up late, sitting around the fire after my uncle had gone to bed. She told me about a man she'd dated, briefly, who styled himself a backcountry camping aficionado while overlooking her expertise. On their first camping trip together, she'd tried not to laugh as he inflated a blimp-size air mattress. She'd spent the night rolling off his mattress and clambering back on while he snored, oblivious. Eventually she had concluded that the comforts that came with a boyfriend simply weren't worth the effort it took to educate him about feminism and consent. I listened and nodded and thought, somewhat sheepishly, about the years Mona had spent educating *me* about feminism. When we'd first met fifteen years ago, I still believed God had ordained me, as a man, to lead my household. I wondered where our culture would be now if a religion that worshipped a dominating male deity hadn't so successfully crushed pagan visions of a divine mother. Was it too late to go back?

The good weather held until the last night of our trip. As we pitched our tents on a rock ridge overlooking a chute of narrowing whitewater, the wind picked up and the air darkened with cold. Slivers of sleet pricked the backs of my hands as I lit our camp stove. In the west, the sun smeared orange on the heavy bellies of gathering clouds. The river below us looked like a channel of fire between walls of rock. We'd had a good run, but the weather had finally caught up with us.

In the morning, snow was coming down in wet clumps. We broke camp and stuffed our gear into our canoes while gnawing half-frozen granola bars washed down with cinnamon whisky. I was soloing my canoe, and it was a long, difficult day of slippery portages, numb fingers, and bitter headwinds. I spent most of it kneeling on sopping mittens and fighting to keep my prow cutting into the wind. By late afternoon the damp had seeped through my rain gear and my fingers felt like limp spaghetti. I didn't know how much longer I could keep a grip on my paddle. My uncle and cousin were up ahead, out of sight. I had no idea how far we were from the end or how many more hours of paddling strength I had left to fight the wind.

And then without warning, the wind dropped away and I found myself alone in a solemn dance of snowflakes descending onto the river's silver pane. The rough trunks of balsam poplars congregated close along the shore. I could feel them watching me, breathing. I'd experienced this before when alone in a forest, a sense that the trees were conscious, observing me from across the species divide.

They were utterly beautiful and strangely aloof. They acknowledged me, but they did not care about me in a personal way. If I died here in the forest, they would take me in; I would become part of them. Like god, like an all-encompassing life force, but without the personal regard or judging vigilance. I was alone but not alone. My spirit and the spirits of the trees were tangled together.

It came to me that it wasn't only the ecosystems of the planet that were facing an epochal shift but our relationship with them. Humans were beginning to reckon with the realization that we had the potential to wipe out not only our own species but many others as well. I was nearly forty. In my lifetime we'd destroyed more than half the wildlife populations on earth. But we had the potential to inhabit this world differently. In that moment on the river, alone with the trees, I knew the crisis we were facing was not just a technological or economic or political problem, it was also a spiritual one. I needed to go in search of another story, a story equal to our moment.

In some ways it was a beginning. But in other ways it was a search I had been on all my life.

Chapter 2

POSSESSED

LIZARD CLAWS SCRABBLE ON the roof. Corrugated metal ticks and pops under the heavy glare of hot-season sun. Inside the four-room brick schoolhouse of my boarding school, five students scrape their pencils reluctantly across the pages of their workbooks. Under my T-shirt, a bead of sweat runs down my ribs. A rooster crows, answered by the imam's midday call to prayer, thin and undulating, rising like a thread of smoke on a windless day. The tremble in his voice makes me want to cry. These days even the most inconsequential things trigger tears: the sun balanced like an orange on the world's rim, the ticklish smell of raindrops hitting dust. Homesickness ambushes me at night under my mosquito net or as I'm brushing my teeth in the dormitory bathroom. The flare of a match makes me think of my father at home in the village lighting lanterns and getting out his guitar to play French worship songs. Tears drip without warning into my breakfast oatmeal. This is an embarrassing condition for a twelve-year-old praying for puberty who anxiously scrutinizes his armpits for hair and measures the girth of his wrists with forefinger and thumb.

On this particular day in 1993, what makes me cry is a fictitious story written by a girl half my age. A girl whose hair is cut short like a boy's and who likes to lay her head down on her books in the middle of class and scowl. It's the last day of school before Easter. Later that afternoon our parents will arrive to take us home for the break. Our teachers have assigned us to write Easter stories, and we take turns reading them aloud. The short-haired girl has written a story about an Easter Bunny who has a conversation with Jesus. Inwardly, I scoff: the Easter Bunny is made of chocolate, and Jesus is the saviour of the world. These two things do not belong in the same story. The girl doesn't want to read her story, so the teacher reads it for her. In it, the Easter Bunny tells Jesus that she is afraid to die. But Jesus tells her he himself has died and there is nothing to fear. Suddenly I feel that awful, familiar burning behind my eyelids. The ocean I've been trying to keep corked has been released.

No one must see me cry, so I run outside. The screen door slams behind me. I take refuge in the thin shade of a flamboyant tree whose petals are the colour of Jesus's blood, and I pin my knees to my chest and knuckle my eyes. I'm crying because I too am afraid to die. I don't want to lose this world. Not today or any other day.

On the edge of the village where my family lives, an artesian well spouts a clear and steady stream from deep within the earth. Clean water is hard to come by. Most of the wells in the village are dug by Nto Dyolo, the old blind man, who sits on the ground with his legs splayed in front of him and chips away at the soil between his knees, shifting his buttocks after every few chops, his heels circumscribing a slow circle as he bores into the earth. But the artesian well is a mystery, a narrow spout emerging from the ground. Who drilled it? What keeps the water flowing? Why doesn't it run out? I feel like an artesian well, a bottomless reservoir of tears.

When my dad arrives later that day, I hug him. He smells like mild sweat and truck exhaust. His beard prickles my forehead. I feel my muscles loosen, and I realize I've been holding them tight since he dropped me off at school six weeks ago.

My sister and I get into the cab beside him, and we drive the ribbon of red gravel to our village. The Peugeot's gears mewl as we descend the long hill into the valley where our village lies, the village to which God has sent us: clusters of mud-brick houses strung out along a creek surrounded by fields of yams, sweet potatoes, sorghum, millet, peanuts, and corn. We pass the half-burnt stump we call a camel and my dad begins to hum "This World Is Not My Home."

My artesian well is flowing again. I put my head out the window and let the hot wind dry my face.

That night after supper I sit on the porch with my mother in a circle of lamplight and we drink sweet tea and I tell her everything I'm feeling.

Write it down, she says.

Why? I want to know. Why should I record this river of sadness?

Because, she says, one day you'll want to remember how you felt.

This does not seem likely to me, but when I'm in my bed I turn up the wick of my lantern and open my exercise book with a yellow mosque on the cover and try to scratch my way toward the crux of my grief:

Almost all my life so far I have been a Christian but God has never seemed very real. I believed in him but I felt like I didn't know him. Mom has always been like my God. Mom always had the answers to my questions and took care of all my needs. I read stories about people talking to God and being comforted by his word. But it seems like God and I speak different languages. When I pray I feel like I am putting a letter into a bottle and corking it up and throwing it into the sea with faint hopes that someone will get it and write back. I never feel like I am talking to someone when I pray. When I read Bible verses I don't really understand them. Whenever I have problems I bring them to Mom because I can talk to her. In a way she is the translator between me and God. If there is a situation where Mom doesn't have an answer and the only solution is to pray, I feel almost hopeless. I have never really realized this until today. Mom says that whoever seeks for God will find him, so I hope that someday I will find God.

A FEW DAYS LATER my dad and I go on an early morning bike ride. The rains have just begun, and the parched savannah is transforming itself into a radiant green. Loose white sand drags at our tires as we climb out of the valley and crest a plateau carpeted with dew-drenched grass and strewn laterite boulders the colour of Mars rocks. The glittering plain saturated in green and red makes my throat seize up again. It isn't the tragedy of the world that makes me weep but its sweetness. How can I endure the knowledge that all of this is temporary? There is heaven, of course, but a secret part of me doubts that the next world could hold a candle to this one. Time itself is a mean trick. Every beautiful scene, every moment of love, is constantly evaporating into the past. Its knife-edged wave carries me toward the rocks.

Eventually I outgrew this desolate phase. My mother credits a book she gave me called *How to Be Your Own Selfish Pig*, written by Susan Schaeffer Macaulay, the daughter of Francis Schaeffer, a leading intellectual voice in evangelicalism at the time and one of the architects of the Christian Right. Illustrated with quirky cartoon drawings, the book tried to provide a logical working-out of Christianity for confused adolescents. Rereading it as an adult, I find its logic blinkered and trite, but when I was twelve the book's common-sense tone and willingness to address my existential questions helped steady my universe on its axis. The artesian well subsided. My trust in the Christian story returned. It comforted me to know I was part of a grand narrative being directed capably by a divine author.

The period of sadness that I went through at age twelve changed my understanding of the world, however: I learned it was possible to question the story I'd been given. I still thirsted for a mystical encounter. I wanted an experience that was more concentrated, more vivid than anything I had known. I wanted to witness a miracle. I wanted the laws of physics to shatter in front of me. Jesus was always bringing people back across the doorstep of death and deflating storms and sending demons screaming into herds of pigs. I had never witnessed such things. No one I knew in West Africa doubted that another incorporeal world intersected with the world we could see and feel and smell. Riding my bicycle to school, I ducked to avoid a warted gourd that hung over the path, certain that if I touched the gris-gris or picked a mango from the tree my skin would break out in a curse of blemishes. One of my schoolteachers said that every time he dreamed of water someone died. In the marketplace a man with dreadlocked hair, pendulous genitals, and a begging tin on his arm wandered naked. People gave him food and warned children not to offend the spirits lest they end up like him. My family swallowed bitter malaria pills with our breakfast oatmeal, but we knew that prayer was the real prophylactic. Illnesses were caused by viruses and bacteria, but even microorganisms obeyed the command of God. When our fickle Peugeot refused to start, our first recourse was always prayer. Sometimes it worked before we even opened the hood.

A book circulated among the missionaries until its pages were dog-eared and tattered. *In Sorcery's Shadow* was written by American anthropologists Paul Stoller and Cheryl Olkes about their sojourn among the Songhay people in nearby Niger. To learn about Songhay culture, Stoller had apprenticed himself to a sorko, a traditional healer. At first he considered his mentor's magical feats to be illusions. But as his initiation took him deeper into the sorko's world, Stoller's secular certainty began to flake away. After a vengeful curse was placed on a visiting foreigner and a member of the man's family fell deathly ill, Stoller became uneasy. Was this power real? One night he woke to find himself paralyzed from the waist down. The paralysis eventually passed once he remembered to recite a protective incantation given to him by his mentor, but the incident left him shaken, convinced he'd been caught up in a real-life showdown between spiritual forces. Eventually he and Olkes fled back to America. Their previously unwavering faith in secular science was gone. My parents and the other missionaries saw the book as proof of what they'd known all along: even secular anthropologists acknowledged that the supernatural was real.

Nevertheless, as fervently as I prayed for a miracle, and as diligently as I tried to muster the requisite faith, I never witnessed anything that I could say for sure was super-natural. Eventually, I decided that the natural order of the universe was the miracle. Humans breathed out carbon dioxide while trees breathed it in. Monarch butterflies navigated by the magnetic pull of the earth. A stranger on a street corner offered directions in a moment of need. God healed people through vaccines and chemotherapy.

But I couldn't quite let it all go. Even serious secular scholars of religion admit that human encounters with the sacred are, on some level, real. I knew that as a child and I know it still, though I have no clear explanation or theory for how it works. I believe in the laws of science. I also believe that people experience phenomena that appear to defy those laws. There is much we do not know.

I MOVED TO CANADA in the summer of 2000. I was nineteen. I'd recently graduated from high school in West Africa and was returning now to my country of citizenship. I lived that summer with my grandparents in Blumenort, a farming village founded by my Mennonite ancestors in the late 1800s on land allotted to them by the Canadian government, land that I now know had been seized from its original inhabitants — Cree, Anishinaabe, and Métis nations — by violence and deceit. I spent the summer at the local sawmill piling fresh-sawn, piney-smelling two-by-fours into neat stacks as the planer spat them out. With the money I saved, I enrolled at the same Bible college my parents had attended. Every student was required to find a place to volunteer as a training ground for the mission field. I picked a Christian drop-in centre in Winnipeg's North End, a neighbourhood I was told was full of spiritual darkness.

The drop-in centre's mission was "to bring hope and a future through Christ to youth and their families in the inner city." At the time, the staff and volunteers were nearly all white. The youth who attended were mostly Indigenous. It was clear who was bringing hope to whom. The centre had been started by a couple of young men who had seen *The Cross and the Switchblade*, the high-adrenalin film based on the bestselling account written by a young Pennsylvania preacher who heard God calling him to bring Jesus to gang members in New York City.

Part of the organization's strategy was to take children out of the city on backpacking and canoe trips. Out in the wilderness, we believed, away from the vices of the city, the children would be open to hearing about Jesus. I led some of these wilderness trips myself. I didn't recognize the incongruity of someone like me taking Indigenous children out for spiritual experiences onto lands their ancestors had held sacred for generations and where settler governments had forbidden them to practise many of their spiritual ceremonies. I knew little about the legacy of settler colonialism in Canada and nothing about the church-run residential schools that had tried to strip a generation of Indigenous children of their culture, identity, spirituality, and sense of self-worth. Nor did I know that other programs for at-risk youth existed in the North End, programs rooted in a culture and spirituality that had been connected to this land for thousands of years.

At the drop-in, I played with the children: pool, foosball, floor hockey, and reckless games of manhunt that started outside under the streetlights on the icy parking lot and spilled into the yards of cranky neighbours. Each evening at the drop-in centre we sat everyone down for

Talk Time, usually a story from the Bible book-ended with admonitions against lying and stealing and having sex and smoking pot. God loved each one of them, we reminded our listeners, regardless of their transgressions, and Jesus was waiting with open arms whenever they were ready. No one was required to stay for Talk Time, but you did have to choose whether you were going to sit inside and listen or wait outside in the cold.

Talk Time always set a minor drama in motion. As soon as the announcement dropped, there were always one or two who seized the opportunity to sow chaos by tearing around the drop-in centre, diving behind the snack counter, snatching canned drinks from the fridge, rolling under pool tables, and locking themselves in bathrooms. A few volunteers would hunt down the renegades while others positioned themselves at the heavy steel front door, ready to slam it shut after they were out. Some nights I'd brace myself against the wall and force the door slowly shut against the resisters while other volunteers shoved stragglers through the narrowing gap. It was like closing a suitcase full of cats.

One night, I ejected a nine-year-old girl I'll call Ashley. She calmly took a seat when Talk Time was announced. But as soon as the door was locked, she jumped to her feet and started dodging around the room while the rest of the children cheered her on. When I finally corralled Ashley, she went limp. I dragged her to the front door by her upper arms. Two volunteers held it open. I was almost there when her body sprang into motion. She tried to twist from my grasp, but I was ready. I locked my grip on her wrists and in a quick brutal motion levered her through the open doorway and out onto the concrete step. The door slammed shut. Outside I heard a sob that morphed swiftly into a laugh. She kicked the door once and ran away into the night. I felt bad. I knew I'd been too rough. But I was doing God's work. Years later, I would find myself standing in front of a Kent Monkman painting depicting RCMP officers in bright red serge and priests in dark robes tearing children from their parents by their limbs and hair, and I would think about this moment.

At the drop-in centre I spent a lot of time with an eleven-year-old boy I'll call Rodney. Rodney had a mischievous smile and spoke with a lisp and was an accomplished car thief. He often arrived home in the early hours of the morning in the back of a cop car. At eleven, he was too young to face charges. Sometimes I drove him home after the drop-in closed to the apartment he shared with his grandfather, a white-haired man with a Polish accent who always seemed to have a cigarette smouldering between trembling fingers. He'd wring his hands and ask me what to do about Rodney. I had no answers, but I sat in his tiny kitchen with its nicotine-yellowed walls and drank the burnt coffee he offered me and stared at a picture on the wall of a svelte white Jesus whose thorn-wrapped heart sprayed beams of light. I believed that Jesus could save Rodney, but I had no idea how to get Rodney into those pale, sorrowful hands.

Late one night I got a phone call from a member of the drop-in staff. She had terrible news: Rodney was dead. He'd been riding in a stolen car while the driver did donuts on an icy parking lot. I could picture him leaning out of the window drinking in the wintry wind the way he did whenever I gave him a ride. One of his companions, watching from the sidelines, had thrown a shovel at the spinning car and it had struck Rodney in the head. The vehicle had stopped and everyone had fled the scene. I lay on the floor of my bedroom and wept. All my efforts to bring Rodney to Jesus had failed. Now it was too late.

The director of the drop-in centre spoke at Rodney's funeral. I don't remember exactly what he said, but I'm sure it was a version of a sermon I heard many times growing up. Maybe God had given Rodney one last chance. Maybe God had frozen time at the instant of Rodney's death. Maybe Rodney had stepped across the divide and into the arms of Christ. I pinched my hands between my knees and stared down at the floor. I knew there was something clearly wrong with a belief system that had to tie itself into imaginative knots to sidestep the cruel logic at its centre.

TWO YEARS LATER I met Mona. We were both university students: I was studying journalism and she was working on a degree in conflict resolution. Like me, she was the child of missionaries. We'd grown up on opposite sides of the African continent, she in Sudan, I in Burkina Faso. She had a long, sunshine-coloured braid that hung down her back, spoke four languages, and enjoyed camping in the desert. The first time we met she plucked a leaf from my hair and a little electric current ran from my scalp down through my feet into the ground. We both signed up for the same class, "The Study of Voluntary Simplicity," taught by a Benedictine-oblate-turned-Buddhist who opened his first lecture by teaching us to meditate on an orange. The class examined the spiritual and environmental reasons why people choose to live lives of material restraint. Neither Mona nor I considered it an academic exercise. We shared a set of used textbooks. This was how we intended to live our lives.

Mona had also been raised an evangelical Christian, but when we met she was already well on her way out of the faith. She told me this in various ways, which I tried not to hear. We had so much in common: missionary childhoods, the struggle to find our places in the world, our efforts to see past the glare of our own privileges. We both lived on our summer earnings, scavenged food from dumpsters, and walked or cycled everywhere. I admired her jeans, salvaged from a thrift store and modified into bellbottoms. Her Spartan library — the Bible, the complete works of Shakespeare, a book of Rumi's mystical poetry — inspired me to cull my own book collection. My university student housemates rolled their eyes. "I could tell by her clothes that you two were going to end up together," one of them said.

Obviously we were meant to be together. But I was also wary. The God I'd grown up with was a jealous God, a God who repeatedly warned the Israelites not to marry women from surrounding nations lest they be lured from his embrace. I wanted God to possess me. I filled my journals with letters asking to be burned up or poured out like an offering to him.

When our rendezvous to share class readings began to devolve into make-out sessions on her futon, I decided it was time to invite Mona out for coffee and ask her what she believed about Jesus. She stared at me in startled silence over our cooling coffees. Then she answered my question with stories. Stories about growing up as a girl under a patriarchal faith. Stories about knowing that God did not love women the way he loved men. God had created women to meet the needs of men, to be homemakers, child-bearers, comfort-givers, and servants. Mona did not want to be any of those things. She wanted to be a human, a doer, a leader, a sexual being. After high school, she'd tried to become a missionary herself. She'd spent a year and a half on a ship named *Logos II*. Stocked with Christian literature, it docked at port cities around the world where the ship's young missionaries would venture out to share the gospel. It was Mona's job to set up the speaking engagements. The preachers were all men, younger than she, and awkward in languages Mona spoke fluently. But she was not allowed to preach because God had not ordained women for that task. So she shelved books in the ship's bookstore and fell in and out of love with men who were looking for obedient wives. When she finally fled the ship, she knew she could never go back to her childhood faith.

Mona's stories tormented me. The day after our coffee date, I wrote in my journal: "I feel like God's given me a beautiful gift, and like Abraham, he's asking me to give it back." I was referring to the Bible story in which God grants Abraham the son he has longed for all his life and then turns around and asks Abraham to sacrifice his beloved son on a mountaintop.

Mona wisely suggested we explore our faith in an exchange of letters. She stitched a sheaf of paper into a notebook and glued a cut-out of a backpack and a camera on the cover to symbolize an expedition. We called it our "collaborative novel" and passed it back and forth, filling its pages with convictions, prayers, and fears, searching for common ground.

"After the ship experience," she wrote in the collaborative novel, "I decided that everything was up for questioning except the existence of the Divine and that I would reconstruct things from there. I am still in the process. And you are so sure of everything. But this is where I am and I can't change that now even if it scares me, scares you, scares us. Do you think that my faith journey and our you-and-me journey can travel together for a while, holding the uncertainty gently, at least until we know that there is a fork in the road?" She quoted Rainer Maria Rilke. She asked me to have patience with everything that remained unresolved within me, to strive to *live* the questions themselves.

How prescient she was.

I knew I should probably end the relationship, but I couldn't. I was enthralled by the poetry of her quest and the fragrance of her scalp. I followed the trail of questions she dropped, like breadcrumbs, coaxing me deeper and deeper into the labyrinth. We continued writing to each other in our collaborative novel, long, searching, sometimes painful negotiations about what we believed and what we didn't. We agreed to live the questions, as Rilke advised.

When we eventually decided to get married, Mona made two things clear: we would not have a head of the household (though my parents insisted our marriage would founder without one), and if we had children, I would be the one to stay home with them. I agreed to both stipulations. I was starting to understand the many ways my faith exerted its power over women, over Indigenous Peoples, over the land. But I still believed Christianity held the tools of liberation as well. Hadn't Christian teaching also fuelled the rebellion of abolitionists and civil rights activists and suffragettes? Didn't every story of Christian domination also come with a story of Christian resistance and solidarity with the oppressed? That was the side I wanted to be on. I volunteered to take Mona's last name. It felt like the kind of symbolic relinquishment of power that Jesus would endorse.

My mother disagreed. "I wish I could say that this is okay, but I can't," she wrote to me in an email. "I suppose you think that there is such a thing as a family without a head, and that yours is going to be one." I didn't argue with her, but I went ahead with the paperwork. I'd grown up in the home of a woman with strong convictions, and now I was marrying another one.

After we were married, Mona finished her education degree while I looked for work. Journalism jobs were scarce, but I found one at an evangelical Christian newspaper. Each week, I browsed headlines looking for news stories that might have a Christian angle we could pursue. Legislation on medically assisted dying, churches splitting over same-sex marriage, shrinking church attendance, the erosion of Christian influence on politics and culture — these were our bread and butter.

Meanwhile, I was doing a lot of reading. I read accounts of residential school survivors abused by the church, Frantz Fanon's searing indictments of colonialism, the speeches of Thomas Sankara, a pan-Africanist revolutionary who had briefly been president of Burkina Faso during my childhood there. Sankara railed against Western imperialism. His speeches resounded with liberation theology: Christ's message of solidarity with the poor and oppressed had been twisted into a club by imperial powers. Four years into his political experiment, Sankara, like Christ, was betrayed by a close friend and assassinated with the help of the very powers he'd rebuked.

I read a memoir by Malidoma Somé, another man from Burkina Faso, seized as a child from his village and forced to attend a seminary run by French Catholic priests. Fifteen years later he'd escaped and walked 200 kilometres back to his village. He'd forgotten much of his language and had missed out on the traditional initiation rites his peers had undergone. "The spirit that animates the whites is extremely restless — and powerful when it comes to keeping that restlessness alive," Somé's father said to him. "Wherever he goes he brings a new order, the order of unrest. It keeps him always tense and uneasy, but that is the only way he can exist…Until he is at peace with himself, no one around him will ever be."

I was tense and uneasy myself. I could feel my faith slipping. Questions rose in me like ocean swells. I read Shusaku Endo's novel *Silence*, about a Portuguese priest who ministers to persecuted Christians in Japan while searching for one of his colleagues rumoured to have renounced the faith. The priest listens for the voice of God but hears only the eternal lap of waves on a darkened beach. I too knew the sound of God's silence.

I attended a sweat lodge ceremony led by an Indigenous elder. I described the experience in an email to my parents: "I'm someone who experiences the presence of God most deeply outside in nature, and I felt that I was among people who had a deep relationship with the Creator, praying to him in way that was truly their own."

My parents responded with alarm. My description of the sweat lodge must have reminded them of the pagan practices they were trying to expunge. I knew they feared for my soul. I didn't yet have children of my own, but I couldn't imagine the terror of seeing my own child teetering on the edge of that abyss. I longed to reassure my parents, but I also knew that I no longer wanted to be possessed.

Christianity wanted everything: women, men, souls, land, wealth, power. In 1572, José de Acosta, a Jesuit missionary from Spain, travelled to Peru and marvelled that God had strategically buried gold and other mineral riches in "the most remote parts of the world, inhabited by the most uncivilized people...in order to invite men to seek out and possess those lands and coincidentally to communicate their religion and the worship of the true God to men who do not know it." Acosta's argument has been recycled by theologians and intellectuals of every colonist nation, African American theologian Willie James Jennings has pointed out, and is reflected in Manifest Destiny and the Doctrine of Discovery, legal frameworks created by European monarchs and still used to justify the seizure of Indigenous lands.

I remember the moment I realized that I no longer believed in the story of the saved and the damned. I was crossing a Winnipeg street. Snow had fallen in the night, and the city lay cloaked in a glittering mantle. I felt like a creature who had awakened mid-hibernation and emerged into a world both familiar and transformed. I stared into the faces of people I passed, luminous and strange. I knew, quite suddenly, that none of us were going to heaven and none of us to hell. All of us — me, Rodney, Thomas Sankara, Malidoma Somé, Mamadou, Mona, the people on the street — were simply wanderers in a tragic and beautiful world. I quit my job at the Christian newspaper and stopped volunteering at the drop-in centre.

It was a beginning more than an ending. Years later, Mona would tell me what she hadn't dared to say in the coffee shop: "When I left the ship, I knew that God did not love me. But I also knew that behind God, there was something much bigger. And that being loved me. The earth loved me."

Chapter 3

EMBATTLED

"WHAT HAPPENED ON TUESDAY night will alter the direction of history and change the world," I wrote in my journal a day after Donald Trump was elected president of the United States. It was November 2016. I'd stayed up to watch election night coverage with my brother-in-law. Neither of us was American, but the U.S. presidential election always offered a spectacle. A spectacle with consequences, both for our country and the planet. This election, we knew, would be more fun than most. We'd get to see the bombastic orange clown brought low and a woman ascend for the first time to the White House. We joked that if there was one thing Donald Trump did not know how to do it was lose. How would he react? I brought beer. My brother-in-law provided the chips. We made puns about glass ceilings.

But as we watched the votes roll in and the states on the map flip one by one from blue to red, our jokes petered out. On CNN, the expression on Anderson Cooper's face clouded from upbeat to incredulous to grave as it became clear that the unthinkable was happening. Eventually we ceased talking altogether, each of us trying to grapple with what we were witnessing. When I finally walked home in the early hours of the morning, my shoes crunching on frost-crisped leaves, my mind didn't seem to be working properly. It would begin to reel out a line of thought, then hit a glitch and jump back to the start.

My house was dark. The children were asleep. I slid into bed against the warm curve of Mona's back. She rolled over to embrace me and mumbled, "Who won?" It didn't feel right to utter his name in the intimacy of our bedroom, but I did, and I felt her body tense. "Seriously?"

"Yes."

She lay still for a few seconds and then rolled away. "Oh my God." She kicked off the blanket and sat up. I couldn't see her face, but I felt her shudder. She got up and walked to the bathroom. I heard the door click behind her, then her gasping sobs.

I knew why she was upset. Our people, evangelical Christians, had chosen this man. Although neither of us still considered ourselves believers, the faith we'd both grown up with had formed our early identities and shaped our sense of responsibility to the world. That this faith could endorse a demagogue, a liar, a racist, a man who boasted about grabbing women by the genitals, sickened us. After Mona emerged from the bathroom, her eyes swollen and red, we went downstairs, poured ourselves bowls of Cheerios, and talked about what would happen next: about the children who would be bullied, the women who would lose the right to make decisions about their own bodies, the people fleeing war and poverty and climate change upon whom hatred would be unleashed, the work toward a renewable energy transformation that would be stalled or reversed. When I finally went to bed in the early hours of the morning, I felt as though the last thread that tied me to Christianity had been cut.

I don't want to give too much credit for my loss of belief to Donald Trump, a man faithless in every sense. My long slide away from the faith had begun years earlier. But his presidency and the knowledge that white evangelicals overwhelmingly supported him illuminated for me with startling clarity how the belief system I had grown up with was hastening the extinguishment of life on earth.

Polls show that white American evangelicals are the only major religious group to largely disbelieve climate science and to oppose action on climate change. Surveys that control for factors such as political loyalties, education levels, and media exposure reveal that a commitment to evangelical Christianity is the trait most consistently associated with climate skepticism. Eight in ten white evangelicals voted for Donald Trump in 2016 and close to that percentage did again in 2020. How did this happen? I wondered. How did a religion that claimed to care for creation and the most vulnerable become such a threat?

As I began to research this question, I learned that there had been a point, relatively recently in fact, when evangelical

Christianity in America had appeared to be on the brink of a conversion, poised to join the struggle for a livable planet. But something had happened to derail that progress.

IN THE DARKENED AUDITORIUM of a luxury hotel in Washington, D.C., on September 23, 2006, an earnest, bespectacled man with short, curly brown hair and a charming widow's peak stepped up to the pulpit. James Inhofe was introduced to his audience of sixteen hundred evangelical Christians as a senator from Oklahoma who travelled the world meeting with heads of state and sharing with them the "political philosophy of Jesus." Flanked by two faux Doric columns and a pair of American flags, Inhofe warned his listeners he had "something very significant" to talk to them about. Only a handful of political issues cut to the marrow of Christian faith, he said. He mentioned homosexuality and abortion, but he was not there to talk about either of these. He was there to warn his listeners about a new front in the battle. Over the next twenty minutes, Inhofe described climate change as an elaborate plot to "shut down this machine called America," a hoax invented by the United Nations and leveraged by liberals and Hollywood elites to destroy the core values of everyone in the room. He played a clip from an interview with an animal rights activist who suggested that assassinating human researchers would save animal lives. He referenced early Christians living under the Roman Empire, worshipping idols and creation rather than the Creator.

The parallel was clear: environmentalists were steering people into false religions. Inhofe urged his audience to fight back. He invited them to join a newly formed coalition of climate-skeptical religious groups and to carry his dire warning back to their churches and the associations to which they belonged. "If you do this, you'll be doing the Lord's work, and he'll richly reward you for it," he said.

Two things were remarkable about Inhofe's speech. The first was the way he positioned environmentalism as an attack on the very heart of evangelical faith. The second was his timing. Inhofe delivered this short speech in the lead-up to the 2006 midterm elections. American evangelicals were at a crossroads. Nearly eight months earlier, a group of eighty-six progressive evangelical pastors and leaders had issued "Climate Change: An Evangelical Call to Action," a statement acknowledging the human causes of climate change and warning that "millions of people could die in this century because of climate change, most of them our poorest global neighbors." The call to action was announced with full-page ads in the *New York Times* and *Christianity Today* and featured in television spots that linked images of drought, starvation, and Hurricane Katrina with climate change. The leaders endorsed federal legislation to limit carbon emissions, and they urged churches to take action.

This was a moment of huge potential within evangelicalism, according to Robin Globus Veldman, a professor of religion and environmental studies at Texas A&M University. "The green movement within evangelicalism was like this significant wave," she told me. "But that wave caused an enormous backlash that came and overtook it."

In 2011 Veldman moved to a small town in Georgia to do field research. She wanted to study how evangelical Christians' beliefs about the end of the world were affecting their views on climate change. She'd become interested in evangelicals while doing her masters' research on radical environmentalists, people who believed society would soon begin to collapse. "I started hearing about evangelical Christians," she told me. "People were saying things like: 'They're the real apocalyptics. They're the ones whose apocalypticism matters for the climate crisis.'" Most evangelicals believe the Bible prophesies Jesus Christ's return to earth. Christ will spirit true Christians into heaven. After a period of upheaval, the earth will be destroyed and unbelievers will be cast into an eternal lake of fire. According to the Bible, droughts, wildfires, and floods signal that these events are drawing near. Veldman expected evangelicals to interpret the symptoms of climate change as signs that the end times were imminent.

For fourteen months, Veldman attended evangelical church services and participated in Bible studies, interviewed pastors, and conducted focus groups with parishioners in the Georgia town she'd chosen. The people she spoke to were deeply skeptical of climate science and even hostile toward the environmental movement. Although polite, her informants ridiculed those who worried that human activity would permanently alter earth's climate. But surprising to her, apocalyptic beliefs didn't seem to factor into people's feelings as strongly as she'd predicted. The evangelicals she talked to did indeed believe that Jesus could return at any moment, but this conviction didn't seem to significantly alter their day-to-day activities. Yes, the world was going to end, but that didn't change their obligation to live faithful lives and safeguard God's creation — given to humans for their use — as long as it was around. Veldman sensed there was a deeper source for her subjects' suspicion.

As she began compiling her research, she turned her attention to the evangelical mass media, a far-reaching network of radio, television, and digital platforms that an estimated one in five Americans reads, watches, or listens to daily. There she found a loosely organized campaign led by figures of the Christian Right to cast aspersions on climate science and the environmental movement. The campaign had been organized in direct response to the evangelical call to action on climate change and a second similar statement that had followed two years later, in 2008, signed by Southern Baptists, the largest Protestant denomination in America.

Conservative evangelical leaders had seen these calls to action on climate change as signs that their hold on a generation of evangelicals was slipping. Many of the signatories were progressive evangelical voices, people such as megachurch pastor Rick Warren and popular author and speaker Brian McLaren, rising stars who challenged orthodox theology and spoke out on social justice issues such as AIDS, Darfur, poverty, and the environment. The old guard of American evangelicalism began organizing a counterattack. In the early 2000s they formed a coalition of religious climate skeptics, the coalition Inhofe told his listeners to join.

Known as the Cornwall Alliance, the group was led by Calvin Beisner, a smiling, goateed Presbyterian church elder with seven children and degrees in religion, philosophy, and economics. Affable, calm, and articulate, Beisner has described his work as "saving the planet from those trying to save the planet." He argued that free-market capitalism had built the prosperous modern world and that the only way to lift more people out of poverty and reduce human suffering was to continue to build and develop. Yes, the climate was changing, but warming and cooling cycles had always been part of the earth's history — these cycles were not under human control. God would look after the weather. The real danger was militant environmentalists who used shoddy science and faulty economics to erode the prosperity of America and the Christian values on which it was built.

Beisner became one of the world's most prominent religious climate skeptics. He spoke at conferences; did interviews on radio, television, and podcasts; penned reports; wrote open letters; and testified before energy boards. In 2011 the Cornwall Alliance published a video series called *Resisting the Green Dragon: A Biblical Response to One of the Greatest Deceptions of Our Day*, which warned that "radical environmentalism is striving to put America and our world under its destructive control." The trailer featured a scaly dragon with a fiery eye straight out of *Lord of the Rings*.

As Veldman analyzed the messaging of this campaign, she began to understand why it was so powerful and persuasive. It touched a chord at the heart of American evangelicalism: their identity as an embattled people at war with secular culture for America's soul.

This identity has deep roots. The seeds of evangelicalism were planted in the decades before the American Revolution, when a series of religious revivals swept through the colonies. Charismatic preachers like Jonathan Edwards delivered sermons about the horrors of hell and urged his followers to make personal commitments to Jesus Christ. This new expression of Christianity emphasized personal conversion and missionary activity, and it spread like wildfire. By 1850 its adherents had doubled to three million. By the beginning of the twentieth century, evangelicals held positions of authority and saw themselves as America's spiritual guardians. But in the following decades, that influence began to wane. Darwinian evolution and biblical criticism challenged evangelicalism's philosophical underpinnings. The horrors of two world wars left many people wondering whether an all-powerful, benevolent God could really exist. As mainline Protestant denominations began to embrace evolution, feminism, and biblical criticism, a group of conservative Christians calling themselves "fundamentalists" set out to return Christianity to the basics. Their name came from a twelve-volume series published in the early 1900s called *The Fundamentals: A Testimony to the Truth*, in which conservative leaders argued that the Bible was literally and scientifically true and a blueprint for human morality. Some three million volumes were printed and distributed for free to ministers, missionaries, theology professors, and religious editors throughout the English-speaking world.

This war against modernism breathed new life into evangelicalism. In the 1920s fundamentalists lobbied state legislatures in an attempt to ban the teaching of evolution in public schools. In the 1940s fundamentalism morphed into the evangelical movement and began to build up a network of churches, seminaries, Bible colleges, mission organizations, publishing houses, record labels, radio stations, and television shows. During the 1970s and '80s evangelicals in America became a powerful political force. They allied themselves with Roman Catholics and the Republican Party to form the Christian Right and fight against abortion and homosexuality, which they saw as stains on America's soul. By the end of the twentieth century, evangelical leaders had made the war with secular culture a central issue to the faith and had mobilized masses to the cause. At one time, scholars of religion had predicted evangelicalism would fade away. In fact, the opposite happened, Veldman wrote in her book *The Gospel of Climate Skepticism*. Under the pressures of modernity, evangelicalism flourished.

Environmentalists weren't always an enemy in this war. Many evangelicals got involved in the environmental movements of the 1960s and '70s in response to oil spills, nuclear testing, and the use of chemical insecticides. In 1970 Francis Schaeffer wrote *Pollution and the Death of Man*, a theological handbook for Christian environmentalists, in which he warned that unless Christians got involved in environmental work, pantheism would be seen as the only religious response to ecological problems and Eastern thought would gain more influence in the West.

But as evangelicals gained power, they were courted by political activists who supported neoliberal free-market economics and who persuaded evangelicals to join them in opposing big government as a way of protecting religious freedoms. This alliance put evangelicals at odds with environmentalists, who relied on federal regulation to protect the natural world. Schaeffer advocated for Christian environmentalism as an *antidote* to Eastern religion, but many evangelicals already suspected the environmental movement of leading people toward Eastern and earth-based spiritualities. It was on this foundation that leaders like Inhofe and Beisner built their case against climate science.

The campaign worked. In 2016, 80 percent of white American evangelicals voted for a presidential candidate who said he didn't believe climate change was real. Four years later, as the next election loomed, Michael Mann, one of the most prominent climate scientists in the world, said without a hint of hyperbole that he didn't believe the planet could survive another Trump presidency.

Joe Biden won the next election with the help of record numbers of young voters worried about climate change. But the threat of Trumpism and the evangelical infrastructure that supports it remains a significant counterforce in the struggle for a just and livable world.

IN EARLY 2022 CANADA witnessed its own Trump moment when a cavalcade of horn-blaring semi-trucks and bearded men waving Canadian flags and "Fuck Trudeau" banners descended on downtown Ottawa. On the day the convoy arrived in the capital, Leon Fontaine,* then pastor of Springs Church, one of Canada's largest megachurches, posted an enthusiastic video to Facebook: "If you've ever felt like the last two years have been an absolute vacuum of common sense and reason, the sheer number of donations and the speed at which this thing has been galvanized just proved that you are not alone!" he declared. "Boy, Ottawa is about to see what 'We're in this together' really looks like!"

For three weeks a belligerent minority controlled the national conversation. By the time riot police cleared the occupation from Parliament Hill, many of the public health measures the protestors opposed had been quietly dropped. As I watched all this unfold, it seemed increasingly evident to me that the religious and political cleavages that had emerged and deepened during the pandemic offered a worrying preview of the religious forces we were up against in the struggle for climate justice.

Christians in the convoy fretted about climate mandates. Pro-oil-and-gas member of Parliament Candice Bergen, propelled to the helm of the Conservative Party during the convoy fiasco, had once been a singer at Fontaine's Springs Church. The Canadian pastors who urged Christians to

* Leon Fontaine died of cancer unexpectedly in November 2022 as final edits to this chapter were being made.

defy public health orders were some of the same ones who hosted Christian climate deniers like Calvin Beisner. Familiar battle lines were being drawn.

During the Ottawa occupation, Fontaine broadcast live nightly chats with two young men in matching side-parted fades whom he'd sent to Ottawa to be "eyeballs on the ground" and show Canadians the "truth" about the occupation on Parliament Hill. "We're hearing people say a bunch of crazy things like it's a political party, it's a this, it's a that, but everybody there, from what I can see, is just on one thought and that is *freedom*," Fontaine told his audience.

In Ottawa, "freedom" smelled like diesel fumes from idling trucks and sounded like a cacophony of air-horns and looked like a lot of shuttered businesses. Paramedics feared for their safety; an ambulance was pelted with rocks; local residents grew haggard after nights with little sleep. But Fontaine's reporters remained upbeat. They focused on the atmosphere of camaraderie among the protestors, the relief of gathering with like-minded people after months of enforced isolation, the nonviolence of the crowds, and the co-ordination of food and fuel. There were barbecues, hot tubs, bouncy castles, and very few masks. "Most people here aren't afraid to uncover their faces," one of them said.

Many in the convoy had come to Ottawa at the behest of God, fighting for their right to trust him with their health rather than government or medical professionals. "Jericho marches" circled the parliamentary grounds, evoking the story in the Old Testament when the Israelites marched seven times around the pagan city of Jericho until the walls fell at a blast of trumpets. One person had brought an actual trumpet made from a steer's horn, though it was unclear whether she hoped to use it to bring down the bricks of the Parliament Buildings or the Trudeau government or just the COVID-19 health orders.

Most churches in Canada had been faithfully following public health orders through thick and thin, and many Christians were upset by Fontaine's support for the convoy. He dismissed the naysayers, likening COVID restrictions to the most brutal repressions of the twentieth century. "I don't know where they get this thing that we should be quiet and say nothing…Go back and look at history… What did Christians do when they were under Hitler, Stalin, Mao Zedong?" he said.

Fontaine began interviewing far-right personalities and conspiracy theorists, posting the interviews on one of his websites called "Return to Reason." Branded as "a common-sense analysis of world events" and a response to the erosion of freedoms and the need for unbiased journalism, the site's landing page played a loop of black-and-white footage featuring Fontaine being dressed and made up backstage like a talk-show celebrity. Among his interviews were anti-immigration member of Parliament Maxime Bernier, a vaccine-skeptical doctor, and a lawyer representing seven churches suing the Province of Manitoba over pandemic health measures.

Fontaine hadn't always been so enamoured with libertarian politics. He pastored Springs Church, whose congregation he grew to be one of the largest in Canada, with a weekly attendance of eight thousand at its three campuses in Winnipeg and Calgary. Before the pandemic Fontaine's Sunday sermons and regular appearances on the Miracle Channel — a Christian television station he helmed — focused mainly on unleashing miracles, cultivating good leadership, and promoting his personal brand of health-and-wealth Christianity called "Spirit Contemporary," a term he trademarked. But something happened during the pandemic to steer Fontaine into the world of misinformation and right-wing politics.

The thread isn't hard to follow.

When the first wave of the pandemic hit, Springs Church shut its doors like everyone else and cancelled in-person gatherings. But it didn't take Fontaine long to come up with a workaround. On March 29, with the pandemic barely two weeks old in Manitoba, Springs held its first drive-in worship service, the show projected onto a screen mounted on a truck in the church parking lot. Eventually this temporary setup was replaced with a permanent LED screen. Soon Fontaine's two-storey face could be seen by cars driving by on the highway Sunday mornings. At first drive-in church was seen by provincial health officials as a safe and creative solution. But six months later, as Manitoba hospitals were being flooded with sick and dying COVID-19 patients, the province prohibited these drive-in gatherings. A few renegade churches in southern Manitoba chose to make flouting public health orders part of their religious identity and kept holding in-person services. Springs continued to hold drive-in services, for which they were fined a total of $20,000.

In August 2021 Jim Hinch, an American religion journalist, wrote an article for the *Los Angeles Review of Books* about the politicization of American evangelicals during the pandemic. He focused on Grace Community Church, a megachurch in Los Angeles. Before COVID-19, its pastor, John MacArthur, well-regarded in evangelical circles, had steered clear of partisan politics. "God left the church on earth to make disciples (not Democrats or Republicans)," the church website stated. At first, Grace co-operated with lockdown orders. But then something happened. The church reopened, defying mask mandates, and was quickly involved in a legal battle with the state. Soon the pastor was being interviewed on Fox News, and Donald Trump called him to offer him one of his campaign lawyers.

"Evangelicals have embraced an explicitly business-oriented approach to ministry that has remade Christianity in the image of corporate America," Hinch wrote. This model was hit hard when indoor worship services were prohibited. Churches that weathered the crisis were the ones that focused on providing pastoral and social services to their congregations and communities. A nearby evangelical church, similar in size to Grace, organized blood drives, served meals, provided childcare for essential workers, and offered technology for families adapting to online school. It followed public health rules without complaint. Meanwhile, Grace, desperate to regain its slipping audience, capitalized on the "freedom" movement. The evangelicals who were loudest in their opposition to pandemic health measures usually came from churches that centred the spectacle of the worship service and the star power of their pastor.

This struck me as an accurate description of what had happened at Springs. Springs Church was built on the brand of Leon Fontaine. He headlined almost every Sunday service, often preaching multiple times in one day. His sermons relied heavily on dramatic stories from his own life. His face beamed at you from nearly every page of the church website, which linked to his personal Facebook, Twitter, Instagram, and YouTube accounts. Fontaine and his wife, Sally, were listed as the church's only senior pastors. Click on "Our Beliefs" and you would get to an ad for Fontaine's book *The Spirit Contemporary Life*. Ushers would hand newcomers glossy devotionals titled "Devoted with Leon." The "with" might as well have been a "to."

Not only did the pandemic threaten Fontaine's business model, it challenged the core of his gospel. Even Christians full of the Holy Spirit, it turned out, could sicken and die of COVID-19 or lose their livelihoods. In this time of crisis he saw an opportunity to restore people's faith in his message by redirecting their fear. The enemy wasn't COVID-19 or climate change. The enemy was public health measures. The enemy was the federal government. The enemy was fear itself. "Faith over fear" became his slogan.

In the spring of 2021 Fontaine preached a four-part sermon series titled "No Deadly Thing." It was based on a verse in the Gospel of Mark that promises followers of Jesus the power to pick up venomous snakes and drink poison without being harmed. "You need to get back into the word of God and begin to believe that no deadly thing — period — is going to hurt you, is going to shorten your lifespan, is gonna attack one of your organs, is gonna make you sick, is gonna stop you from living the kind of life that God has called you to live, which is abundantly!" Fontaine declared from the pulpit.

IN THE SPRING OF 2022 I decided I wanted to see for myself what Fontaine was offering that drew so many people to his church. I was curious about the links between COVID denial and climate skepticism. One chilly spring evening in April, I pulled up at Springs Church, a sprawling boxy building in Winnipeg's industrial outskirts. As I joined the crowd flowing toward the doors, I couldn't help but wonder what each of them had come for. Fontaine had promised miracles but not religion — religion was a bunch of rules. His church was different; he offered power. Miraculous power. "There are a few beacons out there, but most of the churches are dark," he had said. "They don't see miracles on a daily basis."

We could use a miracle, I thought. Antarctica was running a fever of 40 degrees Celsius. The latest report from the Intergovernmental Panel on Climate Change showed a world wholly unprepared for the climate shocks that were coming. UN secretary general António Guterres had called new fossil fuel expansion "moral and economic madness." Somehow, I didn't think that was the kind of madness Fontaine was going to exorcise. I'd heard him complain on television about environmentalists hindering Canada from reaping oil and gas wealth: "If we have all this green thinking in this green movement, if we continue to do this, beginning to shut down oil and gas, go green everywhere we can, Russia, China, all these other countries are not going to do that. Aren't we handcuffing ourselves?"

Inside the sanctuary thousands of people were packed shoulder to shoulder. COVID-19 cases were on the rise again, after a recent lull, but there wasn't a mask in sight. The auditorium lights were low, and the stage blazed with coloured theatre lighting. A troupe of worship performers were rocking out onstage. For the next hour, Fontaine held the room spellbound. Speaking without notes, he told story after story of miracles that he had witnessed and performed. He spoke with the scientific precision of a former medical professional and the timing and suspense of a master storyteller. Shattered bones knitted themselves together and wounds sutured themselves shut under his hands. Corpses he prayed over at accident scenes began to breathe.

The guitars struck up quietly behind Fontaine as he held his hands out over the audience and invited anyone feeling burdened by fear to come forward. "Stop listening to forty-three repeats of the news," he said. "Stop listening to everybody's guess at how bad everything is. You're opening your heart to a spirit of fear ... Fear has gripped you and it's wrapped its tentacles around you and it does not want to let go. And if you don't deal with it, it'll go after our kids, our generations, our families."

The band began to croon: "I feel Jesus. I feel Jesus. I feel Jesus, in this place."

As people swarmed to the front and pooled around the stage, Fontaine, his voice rising to a crescendo, commanded the spirit of fear to "move off in the name of Jesus!" His words were hypnotic. In the spirit of immersive journalism, I tried to set my skepticism aside and enter into the experience. I could feel the knots in my own gut relax as I gave myself over to his voice and let the music cover me like a warm comforting blanket. I was ready for a miracle.

But instead of calling people up onto the stage to be healed, as I'd expected, Fontaine announced that God had "been working on him" and had told him he didn't need to lay hands on people to heal them. He could simply send healing power out over the crowd with words.

With the guitars murmuring behind him, he began to weave a tapestry of commands. "I speak healing right now into the alimentary canal. I speak healing right now into that pelvic cavity. Brains, receive the touch of the Master. Cancer, I command you to take your hands off the child of God! Leukemia, you're a curse, and I command you to come off!" Closing his eyes, he visualized specific ailments among people in the crowd. There was a weird lump behind someone's ear; someone's vertebrae were crushed. "In the name of Jesus, I speak healing into the very bones of that spine," he said, "like a magnet sucking on iron filings, move into place in the name of Jesus right now!"

During his career Fontaine positioned Springs as a beacon in a dim landscape, where Christianity had forgotten its power. But the gospel he preached wasn't new. The prosperity movement was born in America in the late nineteenth century and echoed the optimism of the age. Kate Bowler, a megachurch researcher who teaches at Duke University, calls it "the deification of the American Dream."

So what happens when the prosperity gospel comes up against ecological and human suffering? What happens when the gospel of divine blessing is faced with a disrupted economy, multiplying natural disasters, and geopolitical instability? It turns to a reactionary politics that fights to bring back the good old days when men were men and Jesus was Lord and the economy boomed. Anything that stands in its way becomes an enemy to be defeated.

AS I EXITED THE building into the damp spring evening, I couldn't help but feel cheated. Fontaine had promised us miracles, but I couldn't say that I'd seen one. I didn't doubt that there were people in the audience who felt comforted and empowered by his spiritual optimism — I couldn't deny the power of positive thinking — but what about the people who had come hoping for miraculous healing and hadn't gotten it? COVID-19 couldn't be spirited away any more than climate change could. What if Canada's greatest days weren't just around the corner, but instead we were entering era in which we'd need all hands on deck to care for each other and protect what really mattered?

I remembered a day during the Ottawa occupation when something strange had happened to me. A few blocks from my house in Winnipeg, an army of semi-trucks, jacked-up pickups, John Deere tractors, and house-size flags had taken over a stretch of Broadway under the benevolent regard of the police. Their near-constant honking and aggressively revving pickup trucks were raising my blood pressure. Too wound up to write, I took a walk to the library to clear my head. My route took me past the outskirts of the protest. As I passed a handful of people in snowmobile jackets and baseball caps warming their hands over a fire in a burning barrel, I realized, to my sudden surprise, that I knew something of what they were feeling. I knew the feeling of being powerless against political forces that seemed to be driving everything toward the edge. I knew the relief of finding other people who shared my frustrations. I knew the calm that comes with channelling all that anger into a plan for collective action. I knew the energy of making a visible public statement and the thrill of discovering that people in power were taking notice. I too had blocked streets and occupied politicians' offices and disrupted people on their way to work. The convoy organizers were taking a page out of the playbook of Saul Alinsky, a theorist and community organizer of the political left. But they'd been duped, sucked in by conspiracy theories and misinformation and misled by savvy organizers and preachers capitalizing on people's pandemic frustrations to build a far-right reactionary movement.

A week after my visit, Springs put on a high-quality production of an emotional rock 'n' roll Easter service. "Resurrection power running in my veins," the band wailed as blue and white lightning blazed across the screen behind them. I wasn't surprised that Springs skipped right over Good Friday, a day when Christians contemplate the death and suffering of Christ. Fontaine's God is a God of "Yes," a God of victory, a God of success and healing and wealth, not a God who joins humanity in our collective suffering or shares in the suffering of the earth.

What we need now, I thought, as I made my way out of the Springs parking lot, isn't actually a divine miracle. Let's imagine for a second that Fontaine or the Holy Spirit could suck the carbon out of our atmosphere like a magnet sucking up iron filings. What then? Our economic system would still be devouring the rainforests and wiping out insects and glutting our oceans with plastic. More than a miracle, more than the soothing words of a charismatic pastor, what we needed was transformation.

Chapter 4

BEREFT

IN THE SUMMER OF 2018, as a heatwave scorched the northern hemisphere, causing rail lines to buckle and roofs to melt in the typically cool and rainy British Isles, a British professor published a paper in which he predicted the imminent collapse of human civilization. Academic papers are usually read by no more than a handful of people, mostly other scholars. This one was the exception. Within a year it would be downloaded half a million times. It would cause people around the globe to re-evaluate their lives. Some would quit jobs in academia or finance to become farmers or full-time climate activists. Some would block bridges, glue themselves to windows, or strip naked in Parliament in a bid to get the British government to declare a climate emergency.

The paper's author wasn't some wild-eyed preacher quoting the Book of Revelation. A youthful forty-six-year-old whose round, stubble-salted cheeks dimpled mischievously whenever he smiled, Jem Bendell was a professor of sustainability leadership at the University of Cumbria with more than two decades of experience helping corporate clients, including the United Nations, develop sustainable business plans. The World Economic Forum had named him a young global leader. He'd delivered a popular TEDx talk on currency innovation. Then he'd undergone a personal unravelling.

In 2014 Bendell was promoted to a full professorship at Cumbria. He delivered his inaugural lecture at a literary festival to an attentive crowd. Sauntering back and forth across the stage, he talked about how corporate storytelling could be used to create a truly sustainable future, holding his listeners' attention with sincere anecdotes undercut by wry humour. No one in the audience would have guessed he was on the edge of an abyss. For one thing, he was getting sick.

The day after his speech, Bendell fell ill with the flu. Bedridden he returned to some of the research he'd perused while writing his speech. He skimmed statistics on global poverty and environmental destruction. The numbers were grim. All measures indicated that we were failing to reduce human suffering and protect the systems that supported life on this planet.

In a feverish funk, Bendell followed threads of his research to climate blogs and interviews with scientists studying Arctic ice melt and the release of methane, a greenhouse gas many times more potent than carbon dioxide. Geological records showed the earth had previously undergone five mass extinction events, he learned, each one wiping out much of the diversity of life on the planet. Scientists believed massive releases of methane and carbon dioxide that dramatically altered the earth's climate were responsible for many of these extinctions. The planet was now entering a sixth period of mass extinctions, only this time humans were the ones changing the climate. Reading the data, Bendell came to a pulse-quickening conclusion: humans had already tipped the first domino in an unstoppable cascade of events that would see the collapse of human civilization within his lifetime.

Bendell recovered from the flu, but he was only just beginning his descent into what he later described as "a multi-dimensional experience of loss and of grief." He grieved the suffering he foresaw — for himself, for his family, for humanity, and for the familiar landscapes of his home. He was also grieving a loss of identity and sense of self-worth. Until this point he'd seen himself as an informed, rational, good person working for a sustainable future. He'd sacrificed personal pleasure and leisure time for the cause. But if the world was doomed, all that sacrifice had been wasted.

Bendell began to change his life. He cut back his work hours and resigned as director of the sustainability institute he'd founded. His social circle shrank; whenever he brought up the end of civilization, conversations seemed to fizzle. Dating was exhausting.

At a conference in Australia, Bendell talked about climate change as an unfolding tragedy rather than something that could be solved. He expected his views would alienate his audience. Instead, people came up to him afterward and thanked him for speaking frankly about fears they'd been too apprehensive to name.

In 2017 Bendell took a sabbatical from his teaching job at Cumbria. Over the course of several months, he researched and wrote a paper he titled "Deep Adaptation." The gist of his argument was that global civilization was doomed. Instead of futilely fighting to preserve it, we should begin to prepare mentally, emotionally, and spiritually for its end.

He wrote in blunt, provocative language, avoiding the cautious circumscribed prose of academia. "When I say starvation, destruction, migration, disease and war, I mean in your own life. With the power down, soon you wouldn't have water coming out of your tap. You will depend on your neighbours for food and some warmth. You will become malnourished. You won't know whether to stay or go. You will fear being violently killed before starving to death."

Bendell recommended resilience, relinquishment, and restoration. "Resilience asks us 'how do we keep what we really want to keep?' Relinquishment asks us 'what do we need to let go of in order to not make matters worse?' Restoration asks us 'what can we bring back to help us with the coming difficulties and tragedies?'" People should hunker down, form small collectives, grow their own food, and learn how to make Aspirin on a small local scale, he advised. They should figure out what they would do to secure nuclear sites when they melted down.

Bendell submitted the paper to a journal of sustainable

development that he'd contributed to in the past. The reviewers who read it didn't support Bendell's interpretation of the science, frowned on his theatrical language, and expressed doubt that the article offered "clear contributions" to the field of sustainability. The journal's editor asked him to revise his basic premise. Bendell was irritated though unsurprised. He had, more or less, called into question the entire field of sustainable development.

The University of Cumbria agreed to release "Deep Adaptation" as an occasional paper, one that hadn't yet gone through the rigorous academic review process. Bendell published it on his website in July 2018 with the subhead "The Study on Collapse They Thought You Should Not Read — Yet."

The response didn't come right away. The paper began to circulate by email, mainly among climate activists and scholars. And then everyone seemed to be reading it. In February 2019 *Vice News* published an article titled "The Climate Change Paper So Depressing It's Sending People to Therapy." By then "Deep Adaptation" had been downloaded more than one hundred thousand times.

SOMEONE SENT ME A link to "Deep Adaptation" before I saw the article in *Vice*. I remember reading Bendell's descriptions of methane leaks, crop failures, and survivalists and feeling my skin tighten and my chest cramp. I pictured a world washed in the murky verdigris of the dystopian film *Children of Men*: mangy dogs sniffing at trash fires and human refugees caged in the streets. I felt like throwing up. I wanted to lie down in a dark room and cry.

Like Bendell, I was grieving. I was grieving for the vanishing butterflies and the shrinking forests and for the migrants drowning and farmers stricken by drought. The signs of unravelling were everywhere I looked.

In late 2018 and early 2019, two scientific studies made headlines that ricocheted around social media, startling even the people who had been paying attention. One reported that nearly half the wild animal populations on the planet had been wiped out in the past forty years and a million plant and animal species faced extinction. The other warned what would happen when we reached two degrees of warming, a grim milestone we were projected to hit in the next few decades: four hundred million people worldwide exposed to severe drought, widespread crop failure, the collapse of coral reefs.

One morning in May 2019 I took my young daughter on a bike ride to join a crowd of wilted-looking students standing under umbrellas on the steps of the legislative buildings. Their posters bled marker in the rain: "You'll die of old age. I'll die of climate change." I picked up my daughter and pressed her against my chest. "Why are we stopping here?" she wanted to know. I couldn't begin to answer.

Earlier that morning, I'd logged into an online video forum hosted by Jem Bendell. It was supposed to be a space where people could talk about climate anxiety or feelings of fear and grief as they anticipated societal collapse. The first thing I'd noticed about the meeting was how much it reminded me of church.

Bendell has identified as "post-Christian" and mentioned the influence of Vedic, Jain, and Buddhist philosophies on his spiritual journey. But the participants in this forum were united by something else, a truth that few others were willing to accept: the world was ending. "We are the initiates," said a silver-haired man with a furrowed forehead and small earnest glasses. "We are the ones awakening, and with that comes great responsibility, because as other people awaken, they need — as I needed — people who were awakened before me."

One woman spoke sadly about a rift in her relationship with her adult son. Whenever she tried to talk to him about preparing for collapse, he changed the subject. "We can't change other folks," advised a white-haired woman who called herself a "collapse coach." "If someone is not open to hearing the facts and realities of this predicament, then the most important thing we can do is love them and be present with them." Her words could have been spoken by a pastor from my childhood. I'd heard that sentiment many times before. Love the unbeliever and wait for the truth to dawn. Be there for them when it does.

The end of the world is a powerfully unifying force, something many preachers and cult leaders have appreciated. Some two millennia ago, a Jewish refugee from a failed rebellion against Rome penned a series of visions that depicted the empire's fall with a pageant of characters, including a blood-drunk prostitute, a baby-munching dragon, and a beast with talking horns. John of Patmos's writings were eventually canonized as the final book of the Bible and are still read by many Christians today as a literal forecast for the end of the world.

Bron Taylor, a Californian scholar of religion, has researched the rise of "green religions" in response to the ecological crisis, modern spiritualities with all the hallmarks of traditional religion. The Deep Adaptation forum wasn't a religion per se, but it had many of the features Taylor identified: spiritual elders, common beliefs, rituals of belonging, sacred texts, and grand mythologies.

In the summer of 2020 a group of scientists published a critique of "Deep Adaptation" that found fault with Bendell's interpretation of the data. His predictions of massive methane releases from melting permafrost were based on debunked theories, the scientists said. They warned that "Deep Adaptation" was undermining the climate movement by leading people into paralysis and despair instead of motivating them to do the work that urgently needed to be done to avoid the worst consequences of climate change.

Bendell responded with an aggrieved essay in which he acknowledged some wobbly parts of his argument, but he doubled down on most of it. He was hurt that his critics had focused so much on his paper instead of looking at the movement "Deep Adaptation" had inspired. Bendell amended his paper to clarify that he wasn't *guaranteeing* the collapse of civilization, just putting the possibility on the table so people could talk about its philosophical and ethical implications. He reminded his critics that the paper had been originally written for the business world, people who still thought the world could be saved by tweaking a few corporate policies.

JEM BENDELL ISN'T THE first public intellectual to make predictions about the demise of society. A little over a decade ago, Paul Kingsnorth, a prominent British activist, gave up on the "false hope" of environmentalism, predicted social collapse, and co-founded the Dark Mountain Project, an artistic movement built on a manifesto for "uncivilization" and taking down "myths" of progress, human supremacy, and the separation of humans from nature. In 2019 novelist Jonathan Franzen added his voice to the requiem with an essay in the *New Yorker* subtitled "The Climate Apocalypse Is Coming: To Prepare for It, We Have to Admit That We Can't Prevent It." There are others in the doomsday club, many with even darker forecasts, including Guy McPherson, a biologist and professor emeritus at the University of Arizona, who coined a term I encountered in numerous forums: NTHE — near-term human extinction.

As I thought about these intellectuals, I realized there was something they all had in common: they were all men. Educated, successful, white men near or past the midpoints of their lives. They were seeing cracks appearing in the foundation of a world that had served them well. Their public hand-wringing often coincided with crises of career or personal identity. If there were women out there lamenting societal endings, they certainly didn't command the public platforms these men did. Maybe they were too busy dealing with more immediate needs, like helping find homes for refugees or dealing with family members' mental health crises.

I realized I too had taken a kind of noble pride in anticipating doomsday. While I brooded, Mona soothed our worried children and made space for me to grieve. Societal collapse was less pressing for her than the emotional needs of the people fretting about it.

In the past I would have offloaded some of that burden onto God. But I no longer trusted a divine being to guarantee a good outcome. If God was not saving innocent species from extinction, what were the chances he'd intervene on behalf of a guilty one?

I needed spiritual insight from someone who had actually experienced collapse. Jem Bendell and Jonathan Franzen's climate anxieties were real, but they were still abstract; they hadn't seen their livelihoods destroyed by tropical storms or their homes burned down by a racist settler state or their family members caged at international borders. Why were we turning to them for spiritual wisdom instead of the people living through climate catastrophe right now?

Then I remembered someone who *had* witnessed societal collapse, someone who had walked through the valley of the shadow and left behind footprints of light.

ETTY HILLESUM WAS A twenty-six-year-old graduate student living in Amsterdam when Adolf Hitler invaded the Netherlands in 1940. A Jew, Etty soon found herself banned from shops and public parks, forbidden to ride a bicycle or take the tram. She witnessed friends and neighbours fired from jobs, corralled in ghettos, forced to wear the yellow star, and ultimately rounded up for deportation to death camps. She documented this unravelling in a diary published forty years after her death.

Etty knew she was living in apocalyptic times. Her diary reads like a novel, alive with complex characters and sharply rendered scenes. It documents a piece of history, but it also chronicles a spiritual transformation. In one of her early entries, dated November 10, 1941, Etty's voice is panicked. "Mortal fear in every fibre," she wrote, "Complete collapse. Lack of self-confidence. Aversion. Panic." Eight months later the noose had tightened around her people, but a very different voice rises from the page: "Very well, this new certainty, that what they are after is our total destruction, I accept it. I know it now and I shall not burden others with my fears. I shall not be bitter if others fail to grasp what is happening to us Jews. I work and continue to live with the same conviction and I find life meaningful — yes meaningful…Living and dying, sorrow and joy, the blisters on my feet and the jasmine behind the house, the persecution, the unspeakable horrors — it is all as one in me and I accept it all as one mighty whole."

I'd first encountered Etty when I was in my late twenties, still a Christian but already chafing within evangelicalism's possessive embrace. I was working at the Christian newspaper then, but my personal reading was taking me steadily away from the dogmatists and toward the mystics — Leonard Cohen, Annie Dillard, Thich Nhat Hanh — people who craved mystical intimacy with the divine but were skeptical of doctrines and creeds. Mona and I had moved into the North End, a neighbourhood separated from the rest of Winnipeg by a wasteland of railroad tracks and centuries of racism. We joined a group of earnest white people like us who were trying to start a church for the poor and disenfranchised. Neither of us were interested in saving souls, but we admired the group's efforts to reach across racial and class divides that fractured our city. On Sundays we borrowed a drop-in centre, set out chairs, brewed a pot of coffee, and prayed that someone would wander in off the street. Meanwhile, I was the one spiritually adrift. How could we who had never experienced the slow catastrophes of poverty and colonialism guess the spiritual needs of this neighbourhood, I wondered. I couldn't even guess my own.

I found an English translation of Etty's diary in a used bookstore. Her writing swallowed me like a chill lake on a sweltering day. Here was a soul fully immersed in the spiritual realm yet unconstrained by the strictures of religion. She wrote about sexual and spiritual intimacy in the same breath. She hadn't grown up in an observant family. As an adult, her blossoming spirituality was shaped by meditation and her readings of the Bible, St. Augustine, and Rilke.

Both Jews and Christians have tried to claim Etty, but her spirituality was a thing of its own. She addressed God in her diary, hesitantly at first, but with growing confidence. She never asked God to stop the advance of evil or to rescue her from it. Instead, she asked God to make her into an instrument of consolation. God, to Etty, was not an almighty personality but a presence she found deep within herself: "When I pray, I hold a silly, naive or deadly serious dialogue with what is deepest inside of me, which for convenience' sake I call God," she wrote. Later she elaborated: "I repose in myself. And that part of myself, that deepest and richest part in which I repose, is what I call 'God.'" It was this dialogue with the divine that anchored her, enabled her to see beauty around her, and gave her the fortitude to do the work to which she felt called.

The divine was more than just a facet of Etty's consciousness but a presence that held her. "I feel safe in God's arms," she wrote after her friends urged her to go into hiding, "and no matter whether I am sitting at this beloved old desk now, or in a bare room in the Jewish district or perhaps in a labour camp under SS guards in a month's time — I shall always feel safe in God's arms."

When I'd first encountered Etty, I had been enthralled by her luminous voice and spiritual insights. Now, a decade and a half later, I pulled her diary with its yellow, tattered dust jacket from my bookshelf and opened it again, this time with a different inquiry. I wanted to learn how to live a spiritual life in the midst of turmoil. Her diary entries were still as raw and fierce as I remembered. Her words, flung from the centre of the maelstrom, were still as luminous. I found myself turning to her when I lacked the emotional resilience to read more news about the climate chaos unfolding around me.

That summer, as smoke from wildfires burning the boreal forest in northern Manitoba drifted in a haze over the city, I sat in my backyard and watched a tomato-red sun sink toward a smoky cityscape. Mornings I woke with bars of copper sunlight on my sheets. I took my children on a canoe trip, and we couldn't see the far shore of the lake. My daughter begged to go home. This is the beginning of the end, I thought.

Through it all, Etty's voice steadied me. "This mind is transcendent," I pencilled into the margin of her diary. "No matter what happens, it was worth it to be human." I wanted what Etty had. I tried to pray, but I couldn't address God directly and unabashedly the way Etty did. I'd stopped using words to pray years ago. When I did pray, it was with silence, sitting quietly, trying to let a ray of illumination into my soul or holding someone in the light the way Quakers did.

Etty too hesitated to pray at first, hesitated even to speak the word "God." One day, attempting to pray but embarrassed by the gesture, she knelt in the privacy of the bathroom. "Such things are often more intimate even than sex," she wrote. She told her lover that in sex the body was "the expression of the soul." Eros animated her relationship with the world, even amid the brutality of occupation. "I know the persecution and oppression and despotism and the impotent fury and the terrible sadism," she wrote. "I know it all. And yet — at unguarded moments, when left to myself, I suddenly lie against the naked breast of life and her arms round me are so gentle and so protective and my own heartbeat is difficult to describe: so slow and so regular and so soft."

In her early entries, her emotions seemed to yo-yo between exhilaration and paralyzing despair. Yet as the darkness around her deepened, her inner life moved from chaotic to tranquil. She began to speak to God. She became more sensitive to the intimate beauty in ordinary moments. She still experienced periods of fear, uncertainty, despair, but underneath those emotions, she was calm, confident of her place in the universe. On the morning she found a letter in her mailbox that might be her call-up notice from the Nazis, she quieted herself: "I shall allow the chain of this day to unwind link by link, I shall not intervene but simply have faith."

That sentence struck me. Had I ever allowed a day to unwind freely without trying to impose my will upon it? Every word I wrote was an effort to change the world. I was trying to teach my children how to be good and responsible and sensitive and justice-minded humans. I wrote letters to my representatives in government and helped organize demonstrations in the streets and swept my kitchen floor. Every cup on the counter had to be washed before I could go to bed. On the wall next to the kitchen sink I'd taped up a slogan cut out from the back cover of a rad magazine: "Everybody wants a revolution. Nobody wants to do the dishes." I wanted both. My kitchen counter was something I could control. It was my duty to intervene, to bring order to the world, to alter reality, to do everything in my power to help steer us from catastrophe.

IT WAS TOO MUCH. Without the stabilizing confidence that God would fix things, I had come to believe it was all up to me. I alone could save the world. That was ridiculous, of course, but it was how I felt. I needed help. I needed a guide or a new set of tools.

Mona suggested I see a spiritual director. A spiritual director is like a counsellor for the soul, a guide on your spiritual journey. The discipline has ancient roots in Christianity and Buddhism, but not all spiritual directors are religious. A friend recommended a woman named Ulla. I'd tried to see a spiritual director a few years earlier, but it hadn't worked for me. The man I'd met with had been earnest and eager to help. He'd reminded me of the bearded psychologist played by Robin Williams in *Good Will Hunting*. I hadn't minded the candles or the carved Celtic crosses that filled his study, but he kept bringing Jesus into our sessions. It felt like going for coffee with a friend, only to find he'd invited my ex. I tried to explain to him that, though I thought very highly of Christ, even esteemed him, we'd agreed to see other people.

Ulla was in her fifties. She had short curly hair with blond highlights, an easy smile, and rimless glasses. I thought of spiritual directors as monastic types who wore homespun clothes and rode creaky bicycles, but Ulla lived in the suburbs and drove a red Volvo convertible with vanity plates. The first time we met, in her carpeted basement lined with Buddhas, I struggled to articulate what I was looking for. I hadn't been sleeping well. My mouth kept drying up. I felt like I was running short of breath. Ulla had a solid, grounding presence that quieted something in me. She'd grown up as a German Catholic but had left the church to explore more mystical spiritualities. She understood both the disorientation of leaving one's childhood faith and the longing that remained for a spiritual path.

I told her I was frustrated. I didn't trust myself to find the way. Some part of me still believed I ought to have a belief system that was complete and self-contained to replace what I'd given up. Ulla reassured me that I was exactly where I was supposed to be on the road. Like Rilke, she encouraged me to be patient with myself, to let the tender buds of my new spiritual identity unfurl at their own pace. Spirituality wasn't something you could pursue or seize. You had to let it stalk you. She encouraged me to spend time among trees.

I started seeing Ulla once a month. We would begin our sessions with ten minutes of silence, then talk about whatever was troubling me. I told her I felt most spiritually alive among the rough-barked cottonwoods along the Assiniboine River or the quiet snow-clad pines of the boreal forest. At the same time as I was finding the divine in the world around me, I was also discovering just how embattled she was. Nietzsche had declared God dead, but it seemed to me we were still busy killing her. "Climate change is too big for you to face alone," Ulla said. "Individuals are not made to reckon with something this vast. You're trying to carry it by yourself. Like Atlas with the earth on your shoulders. Can you find a way to shrink the horizons of your grief, to mourn the losses closer to you, but lighten yourself of the burden of the entire planet?"

I tried to improvise a new spiritual practice for myself. I lit candles and read Mary Oliver and took walks among the trees on the riverbank near my house.

"I hate to be the one to tell you this, but you are not in control," Ulla told me in one of our sessions. "You are not in control of your kids, of your life, of the world." She smiled impishly. "I used to think I was in control when I was younger too. I'm not saying that what you *do* doesn't matter. It does. You do what you have to, but then you come up against something immovable. Then you have to accept that you are scared. Accept that vulnerability."

"But I have to fix this," I argued. "I have a moral obligation to move reality in the right direction."

Ulla laughed. "*Move reality in the right direction.* You might want to write that sentence down to see what it looks like on paper."

She was right. I was trying too hard. Maybe I didn't need to stop climate change or believe in God so much as I needed to simply open myself up to something that was already there within me.

"Pay attention to the movement of Spirit," Ulla said.

What was "Spirit," I wanted to know. "Spirit is an invitation from something that loves us deeply," she said. "Spirit will not fix things. Climate change is bigger than you or me. We may not be able to stop it. But I do believe if we listen to Spirit we will live a better life."

I tried to pay attention, to look for Spirit in my body, in

the world around me, though I still wasn't quite sure what I was looking for.

Early one morning I walked the short block from my house to the Assiniboine River. I sat next to its curved brown body and let the sunlight bounce up off the water into my face and shimmer on the grooved trunks of cottonwoods. A pair of mallards came in low, wingtip to wingtip, and splashed down. A rabbit nibbled on some grass. I listened to the shrill descending notes of a white-throated sparrow and the stutter of a woodpecker nailing an elm. I felt something I couldn't describe except to say that it felt like sinking into a cushion of moss. Was this the earth loving me back?

That gentle feeling of being held stayed with me as I walked back home under the cathedral-arched elms shading my street even though I knew the trees were doomed. Each fall city workers sprayed orange dots on a few more of their lovely trunks. Dutch elm disease — a terminal diagnosis. Then the workers in reflective orange vests arrived with their bucket trucks and woodchippers. Eventually all the elms would be lost, but right now, here they were, my companions.

I passed my neighbour, a shy man, out for a walk with his bulldog. His thick-chested canine tried to leap on me, slobbering, delirious with life. My neighbour yanked its leash apologetically. "I never had children," he said. "This is why." I thought about my own children. Each unruly child is a gift. Each disorderly dog. Each troubled human. Each doomed tree. Each hungry elm bark beetle.

Now when I picked up Etty's diaries, it wasn't her grand statements about reality that stayed with me but the small observations of beauty or contentment: the bouquet of orchids hanging over her lover's bed, Amsterdam's soft evening hues, the tree outside her window "heavy with the fruit of stars." The ordinariness of these scenes comforted me. Even in the midst of disaster, there would be tenderness and lovemaking and cups of coffee.

Etty had not only endured suffering, she had opened herself up to it. Her openness to beauty was necessarily an openness to heartbreak. It came to me that Etty's embrace of life and of death were two sides of the same coin. "The reality of death has become a definite part of my life," she wrote, "My life has, so to speak, been extended by death, by my looking death in the eye and accepting it, accepting destruction as part of life and no longer wasting my energies on fear of death or the refusal to acknowledge its inevitability. It sounds paradoxical: by excluding death from our own life we cannot live a full life, and by admitting death into our life we enlarge and enrich it."

The way she wrote about making space for sorrow took my breath away: "If everyone bears his grief honestly and courageously, the sorrow that fills the world will abate. But if you do not clear a decent shelter for your sorrow, and instead reserve most of the space inside you for hatred and thoughts of revenge — from which new sorrows will be born for others — then sorrow will never cease in this world and will multiply. And if you have given sorrow the space its gentle origins demand, then you may truly say:

'life is beautiful and so rich. So beautiful and so rich that it makes you want to believe in God.'"

On September 7, 1943, Etty and her family were put on a train to Auschwitz. She died there three months later.

REREADING ETTY HILLESUM MADE me less bothered by Jem Bendell. His science might have been wrong and his confidence annoying. His writing might even be dangerous — I had seen how quickly the pendulum could swing for some people from "there's no problem" to "there's no hope." In fact, there was hope, and it was vital to keep working for the world we could still save, the future we could still create. Nevertheless, Bendell had done something important: he had helped people to acknowledge their grief.

"Give your sorrow all the space and shelter in yourself that it is due," Etty wrote. This is the spiritual task before us, I thought as I turned the last page of her diary. It is our hardest and our greatest work: to learn to love the world as it is dying and as it is living. To accept the mystery of life and the mystery of death. To go on making love and kneeling in the intimacy of prayer and drinking each cup of coffee with reverence. Once we can do that, we will have the clarity of soul to know what we must do next.

Chapter 5

WILD

ONE LONG-SHADOWED EVENING IN June 2019, a setting
sun and a horned moon shared the sky over a forested hill
amid the cornfields of southwestern Wisconsin. In a clearing on the hill's shoulder, a circle of beings sat around a
snapping bonfire. One by one, they introduced themselves:

"I am a sycamore tree in the Allsopp Forest, and I speak
on behalf of all the trees in the Little Rock area."

"I am honeybee. I speak on behalf of the bees and insects
of the world."

"I am the salmon of the Salish Sea."

"I am giant kelp. I speak for the kelp forests of California."

The beings assembled around the fire were, in fact,
pastors, priests, and lay leaders from churches across
Canada and the United States — United, Anglican,
Episcopal, Lutheran, Catholic, Mennonite, and non-
denominational. They were acting out a ritual designed
by Joanna Macy to "give voice to the suffering of our world."

Each member of the circle spoke from the perspective of a creature or landform native to their watershed and came bearing a message for their human listeners. Each one, after speaking, dropped their persona and took a seat on one of the stumps arranged in the centre of the circle, ready to listen to the next creature.

A few kilometres to the west, trees along the Mississippi River were up to their necks. The river was swollen far beyond its banks and had been for two hundred days and counting. To the south, people were shovelling mud from their houses, and farmers were writing off $4.5 billion worth of corn crops. A warming planet had helped trigger the most catastrophic floods the Midwest had yet seen.

Around the fire, everyone knew things were off kilter.

"We meet in this council because our planet is in trouble," said the leader, speaking with a solemn, measured cadence. "Our lives and our ancient ways are endangered. It is fitting that we confer, for there is much that needs to be said, and much needs to be heard." A United Church minister from Ontario, she wore knee-length jean shorts and a floppy sun hat, and had doused herself in organic vanilla-scented insect repellent to keep away the biting gnats.

The church leaders around the circle belonged to a loose affiliation of congregations known as the Wild Church Network. None of the ministers would return to a building. Not because of flooding but because Wild Churches don't have buildings. They meet outdoors, even in winter. They do this because they believe trees and birds and rivers and stones are sources of divine revelation, just as much as the Bible or the saints.

"We are at a turning point in our culture," Victoria Loorz, a cofounder of the Wild Church Network, told me later. "A turning point defined by ecological destruction as well as societal and ecclesial ending." She believes that if humans hope to survive on this planet, we will have to find a new, more compassionate and interdependent way of living with the species around us, a shift Buddhist eco-philosopher Joanna Macy called "the Great Turning." The Wild Church, Victoria said, is helping birth that new way of being. "We see this as a reformation," she said.

One Wild Church convenes in a beech grove in New Hampshire, another among the cedar pillars of British Columbia's coastal forests, another on the Colorado grasslands. But these aren't just novelty settings for worship. Sometimes the Wild Churches gather on landscapes desecrated by humans: next to a salmon-spawning stream choked with logging debris or a sun-scorched asphalt parking lot or a graveyard of charred trees. They do so in postures of penitence and grief over a broken relationship in a communion that includes humans, the earth, and God.

IN THE WEEKS BEFORE I attended the Wild Church gathering in Wisconsin, I'd been feeling unmoored, adrift, a ship tossed about on the waves of my own emotions. Anger would boil up from within me without warning and spill over onto my children. I'd catch myself yelling at them for not getting their snowsuits on fast enough or leaving a car door open or getting toothpaste on the sink. Why was I yelling? What was wrong with me?

I listened to a podcast about anger. Learn to care for your anger like a small child, said Thich Nhat Hanh. How was I supposed to do that? I was furious over suffering and injustice and the structures of capitalism and wealth and racism exploiting the vulnerable and killing the earth for profit. I was angry at myself for my inability to fix it all.

I brought up anger with Ulla. "I'm a shitty parent," I said.

A little smile played across her face, the smile she indulged in whenever I made an especially dramatic statement. "Anger is just energy. It's not a sign of badness," she said. She encouraged me to pay closer attention to my body, to look for signs of anger about to erupt. "Find the pause between feeling your anger and acting on it," she said.

At the time, I was writing a series of columns about the climate crisis for a spiritual magazine. Each month I'd interview someone working on climate justice and ask them about their spiritual grounding. One person I spoke to, Laurel Dykstra, was an Anglican priest from Vancouver who had spent a week in jail for protesting an oil pipeline in solidarity with a coalition of Coast Salish nations. At the hearing, the witnesses Laurel had chosen to call were "saints and ancestors; endangered, locally eradicated, and extinct species; victims of climate catastrophe." It was Laurel who told me about the Wild Church Network. Their first gathering was in a couple of weeks. I was intrigued.

My initial plan was to attend the gathering as a journalist, not as a participant. But when I emailed Victoria Loorz, she was hesitant. She wasn't sure everyone would appreciate an observer taking notes at the very first Wild Church gathering. The network had come about organically. Many church groups had been experimenting independently with outdoor worship and had discovered each other by word of mouth over the past couple of years, thrilled to find others thinking along the same lines. Almost everyone would be meeting each other for the first time. Instead she suggested that I participate like everyone else. "Who knows," she said, "maybe you'll go home and start a Wild Church in Winnipeg." I smiled at her suggestion, but inwardly I cringed. As much as I liked the idea of a Wild Church in Winnipeg, I had no desire to lead anything religious.

Yet some creature inside me did perk up. That creature yearned to worship among trees, even to exalt the trees themselves. As a university student, I'd spent six summers replanting logged forests in northern Ontario. I could still remember standing at the sheared edge of a forest where a wall of mature pines, shaggy with needles, sprang up from the splintered wreckage of the cutblock. It was an otherworldly verge, a place where it was easy to imagine hosts of the dead raised from the soil by the last trumpet, foliaged and alive. Sometimes I'd unbuckle my planting bags and step through that magical plane into the still-breathing sanctuary of the forest and lie down on a mattress of moss and stare up at the points of pines pinned against the enamel sky. There was nowhere I felt more alive.

I rented a tiny fuel-efficient Chevy Spark in Winnipeg

and set out on a twelve-hour drive to a spiritual retreat
centre run by an order of Dominican Sisters on a wooded
hill in southwest Wisconsin where the Wild Church gathering was happening. The hill had once been home to the
Meskwaki People, who called the area *Manitoumie*, meaning "the land where the Great Spirit lives," before the U.S.
military forced them from their home and built a fort on
the hill. Later an Italian missionary priest purchased the
hill from the U.S. government and founded the order of
Dominican Sisters. For the drive to Wisconsin I borrowed
an audiobook of *Fields of Blood*, Karen Armstrong's
four-millennium journey through human history, from
the *Epic of Gilgamesh* to the events of September 11, 2001,
in search of an answer to whether religion was to blame for
human violence. Her calm, erudite voice carried me over
the border and through looping interchanges and across the
mud-brown sea of the Mississippi. By the time I arrived in
Wisconsin, we'd only just reached the Crusades, but already
Armstrong's bias was clear: she believed compassion and
empathy were the enduring fruits of religious faith, more
than violence, which resulted from agrarian civilization,
empire, and industrialization. I wanted to believe it. Yet,
here in Trump's America, I wondered whether religion and
empire could ever be separated.

Around the fire, a couple nights later, as we acted out the
Joanna Macy ritual, a family therapist from California with
short blond hair and oak leaves tucked behind her glasses
spoke for Grandmother Oak, five centuries old, the oldest
oak in the Ventura River watershed, burned to death in

2017 by a fire that devoured 280,000 acres of forest. "I laid in ruins," she said, "my main branches splayed on the ground in three directions, smouldering for weeks. Older than colonization, I was not able to survive the Thomas Fire, a beast spawned by climate catastrophe, human hubris, and carbon addiction. *Kyrie eleison.*"

"I am the Appalachian Mountains," said a skinny West Virginian with round glasses and a swoop of chestnut hair that kept falling into his eyes. "We once knew ourselves as the world's most diverse hardwood ecosystem." Then came humans, who built roads and gashed the mountainsides to extract coal. "Violent scars cut into our body. Our clean streams ran black. We ask that you would care for our bodies like you would care for the body of your lover. That you would know our bodies like you would know the body of your lover. That you would be gentle with our bodies."

The sun dipped behind the treeline, stealing the gilding from a row of maples and oaks. Overhead, the blue sky darkened. Bats flickered. Snowflakes of ash drifted onto knees and shoulders. I squirmed on the wooden bench I was sharing with Grandmother Oak, hoping I could avoid speaking. Everyone else around the circle seemed to have a biologist's knowledge of their region and a preacher's performative powers. I hadn't prepared any animal story to share.

I'd liked the Wild Church folks as soon as I met them. They were enthusiastic about their faith but not in a way that made me feel like an outsider or that I needed to share their beliefs. They acknowledged other spiritual traditions and recognized the ways those traditions had influenced and enriched their own. During our first supper in the retreat centre cafeteria, I sat across the table from Stephen Blackmer, an Episcopal priest from New Hampshire who had spent the first three decades of his career as a forest conservationist. At age fifty-two, burned out and despairing over the impact of climate change on the New England forests he'd spent a lifetime protecting, he heard a voice telling him to become a priest. The first time he read the Bible, he noticed the trees: from the Tree of Knowledge in Genesis to the tree of crucifixion to the Tree of Life in Revelation. Blackmer anticipated a period of intense suffering for all life on earth. He wanted to be ready to bear witness to it on a spiritual level, like a monk tending a candle during the Dark Ages.

The Wild Church people were convinced that as much as the church needed to regain an environmental lens, so too did the environmental movement need a spiritual grounding to sustain itself over the long haul. Victoria had spent years travelling North America, attending climate rallies with her son, Alec. He'd been twelve when he watched Al Gore's *An Inconvenient Truth*. Almost overnight he'd become a child activist. As a young teen, he led a campaign to sue all fifty state governments for inaction on climate change.

But, after six years of travelling and speaking, both Alec and his mother were exhausted. Victoria said she'd seen the same thing happen with other young people. They'd been full of energy at first. But once they'd understood the true scale of the crisis they were up against, many of them realized that nothing they ever did would be enough. I recognized the feeling.

Spirituality could sustain people for the long term, Victoria believed, even when the outcome of their actions was far from clear. Activists needed to develop "a deep connection to the earth, a kindred, loving, reciprocal relationship with the land and creatures and waters and place that holds you while you do what you're called to do." If you learned to love the earth, Victoria said, you would go on caring for it as you would a dying parent, not because you thought you could save her, but because you loved her. "The cosmology of a saviour who will rescue us from this earth is not sufficient for such a time as this," Victoria told me.

The Wild Church folks understood that Indigenous spiritualities hadn't lost their connection to the land the way Christianity had, but they were cautious about borrowing elements from them without permission, conscious of Christianity's long history of stealing from other cultures. Earlier in the day, I'd attended a workshop led by Laurel Dykstra under a maple tree. Laurel wore Birkenstocks, a bulky pair of camouflage cargo shorts, and a charcoal T-shirt decorated with a teal squiggle made up of two gender signs and a deer antler. "Wherever two or three are gathered," Laurel began, opening with familiar words from the Gospel of Matthew. "Wherever two or three are gathered, there we have sexism and racism and power dynamics."

Gesturing with a tattooed arm at the trees around us, Laurel spoke about "knowing our own stories in the context

of colonization." Laurel spoke with the rhythmic cadences
of someone skilled at turning everyday events — eating,
walking, seeing — into small moments of ritual. Laurel's
was a confident voice but one that asked for respect rather
than commanding it. "Why might you want to listen to
me? Because I screw it up all the time. One example: Often,
after participating in ceremony with Indigenous people, I've
had the desire to take the special or sacred object to have
a souvenir to put on my altar. And the teaching I get from
elders is: 'Put that down! That leaf, that rock, that branch
has done its work and needs you to let it go.' Hanging on
is causing harm. It's the thing that colonists do."

SITTING ON THE BENCH with these tree-hugging
Christians, listening to their laments, I felt their yearning
to disentangle their tradition from centuries of dominion
and colonization and anthropocentric ego. Thomas Berry
had advised Christians to put the Bible on a shelf for a
while until they learned to see revelation in the universe
around them.

I wanted to believe that the Wild Church was a sign of
Christianity emerging from the cocoon as something new
and beautiful and alert to the crisis at hand. But I wasn't
sure if the Wild Church movement alone could slough off
centuries of dominion.

Recent studies showed Christianity, globally, had scarcely
greened its theology since 1967, when historian Lynn White
Jr. described Christianity as "the most anthropocentric

religion the world has seen." Nor had churches taken significant action to address biodiversity loss or human carbon emissions. Although many versions of Christianity had complex theologies about creation and human responsibility to care for it, their responses to the ecological crisis were often relegated to a category called "creation care" and tended to involve book studies or neighbourhood clean-ups or the greening of church parking lots — all good things, but much easier and less political than the complicated work of supporting Indigenous land defenders or advocating for open borders or pressuring governments to stop building new fossil fuel infrastructure. In spite of some hopeful signs, such as Pope Francis's 2015 climate change encyclical *Laudato Si'*, in which he characterized human abuse of the earth as violence against our mother, the old ideology seemed to still be largely hanging on.

JUST BEFORE THE COUNCIL around the fire, I'd participated in another ritual led by Victoria. She'd instructed each of us to go out and find a living thing to listen to. I wandered away from the group and eventually found myself sitting at the foot of a towering oak, curved like a giant bow. It was starkly dead. Its knotted branches, bone-white and stripped of bark, ended in blunted, broken fingers. Its trunk was already tilted toward the ground, where it would eventually lie. A spaghetti tracery of insect paths riddled its wood. Mushrooms had colonized the trunk, green and white, arranged in tiers like balconies on a high-rise apartment complex. An eruption of tiny violet mushrooms bubbled from a white gash in the tree's flesh. The tree was being devoured from the inside out. In death, it fed other lives. My eyes followed its arc upward to where the lowering sun lit the topmost branches. A craggy saint, it seemed to be saying: "Look at me. I am beautiful, even in death." I sat in the grass and touched the tree's body. I felt, in that moment, a strange impulse. I leaned over and kissed the tree, pressed my warm living lips against its dry, barky, dead ones. I smelled its dusty fragrance. I thought that I could love this tree and it could love me back, even in death. Victoria had spoken of a reciprocal relationship to the earth, of knowing that you were loved and held by the earth itself. I longed for that kind of communion.

I also longed to be part of a community like the Wild Churches, a community of people who loved the earth, who felt her suffering on a spiritual level, who reached for the new story that Berry gestured at. But the words that kept bouncing around in my skull as I sat under that rotting oak were, weirdly, not some call to wilderness worship but a line crooned by Ted Neeley as Jesus in the 1970s rock opera *Jesus Christ Superstar*. I could see him with his windblown hair and a fraying flower-child robe, hear his earnest quaver singing Tim Rice's lyric spin on Jesus's paradox: To save your life, you have to give it up. Cheesy, yes, but also as true as anything I could think of right then. I wondered if Christianity still had some dying left to do before it would be ready to rise again with its roots deep in the earth.

Later, around the fire after all the creatures had spoken, someone brought out a hand drum and began beating out a weird wild rhythm that Alec Loorz wrapped in the winding melody of a wooden flute. "Look at the bats," someone said. A few people got up to pirouette on the grass. The music continued, throat-tighteningly beautiful and mournful and sad. Gradually the tempo increased, the notes sharpened in their urgency, the melody rose above the humans, above the biting gnats, above the oak trees to dissipate in the evening sky. Crickets chirruped. Bats squeaked.

"Stay or go, as you wish," said the leader of the circle. "The night creatures will keep singing. With or without us."

Chapter 6

KINDLED

A HELICOPTER SQUATTED LIKE a gleaming black wasp at one end of a snow-covered bridge spanning the blue-green glacier-fed waters of the Wedzin Kwa river. Across the bridge from the helicopter, Freda Huson, a member of the Unist'ot'en house of the C'ilhts'ëkhyu (Big Frog) clan of the Wet'suwet'en people, waited, drum in hand, a ceremonial blanket adorned with crests of her nation across her shoulders. She struck her drum with vehement strokes. "You are trespassing!" she screamed at the helicopter as black-clad RCMP officers dismounted and approached a plywood barricade across the centre of the bridge. "You don't have consent to enter our territory! You are invaders!" Her voice cut through the glittering winter air. Freda's sister, Brenda Michell, stood at her side, striking her own drum in unison. Other women yanked tarps from a wood pyre draped with a Canadian flag, its maple leaf dripping with painted blood, and set the pile ablaze. White smoke billowed over the icy waters of the Wedzin Kwa. Police stood at the barrier for a while and eventually, stymied in their attempt to talk to the Wet'suwet'en matriarchs, returned to their helicopter and stuttered away over the trees.

This is "a cremation ceremony for Canada," Freda declared after they were gone. She held a piece of paper over the blaze. It was a copy of an injunction the British Columbia courts had issued empowering the RCMP to arrest Freda and anyone else who impeded Coastal Gaslink from building a natural gas pipeline across Wet'suwet'en land. "The defendants may genuinely believe in their rights under Indigenous law to prevent the plaintiff from entering Dark House territory, but the law does not recognize any right to blockade and obstruct the plaintiff from pursuing lawfully authorized activities," the judge had written.

"Here's your effing injunction!" Freda shouted after the helicopters. "This is all it's worth: the paper it's written on!" She threw it into the fire.

Half a continent away, I watched on social media. It was February 2020. The pandemic was still oceans away. The previous morning, in the dark hours before dawn, squads of RCMP officers armed with assault rifles, dogs, and drones with infrared sensors had raided another encampment of Wet'suwet'en land defenders along the same road. Police had smashed the windows of a truck and dragged out a woman who had locked herself inside. Six people had been arrested. Images from the raid circulated on social media. The sight of police with dogs and assault rifles removing Indigenous people from their land in handcuffs had made me weep, both for them and for me. The Wet'suwet'en were waging an age-old struggle to protect their territorial rights, but they were also fighting for the rest of us. Our elected officials knew full well we were in a climate emergency. Yet they were still signing off on new pipelines, new tar sands mines, locking in a future of compounding catastrophe. It seemed that the only people with the tactics, grit, and spiritual conviction to defy the forces herding us toward the cliff were Indigenous.

The Wet'suwet'en are only one of many hundreds of Indigenous communities around the world on the front lines of the ecological crisis, both in terms of experiencing the effects of climate change and in resisting its advance. Take a map of all Canada's tar sands, mines, pipelines, and toxic waste sites and lay it on a map showing the places where Indigenous people live and you'll see a shocking juxtaposition, said Clayton Thomas-Müller, a Cree environmental campaigner. The root cause of Indigenous Peoples' trauma is dispossession from their land, he told me. That dispossession is ongoing, led by extractive industries and facilitated by the state.

Indigenous-led resistance to fossil fuels is one of the few strategies whose impact on carbon emissions can actually be measured. Through a combination of civil disobedience, blocking pipelines with their bodies, and advancing claims to their sovereign territories in the courts, Indigenous-led campaigns across this continent alone have prevented or delayed an astounding 1.8 billion metric tons of greenhouse gas emissions from entering the atmosphere during the last decade. Two major pipelines projects, Keystone XL in the United States and Northern Gateway in Canada, have been cancelled by governments in recent years thanks to fierce resistance from Indigenous communities in their paths. In 2020 Teck Frontier abandoned plans for the largest open-pit tar sands mine in the world after sustained resistance from the Dene Nation and other Indigenous groups. Meanwhile, the Gwich'in people in Alaska successfully secured a temporary moratorium on oil and gas development within the 6,000-square-kilometre Arctic National Wildlife Refuge. These are only a few examples.

One report that gathered case studies from every inhabited continent found that lands managed by Indigenous Peoples in the Amazon basin and elsewhere have lower deforestation rates and protect more biodiversity than lands managed by the state. Around the world, Indigenous communities, whose identities and governance systems are deeply rooted in their relationship with the land and other species and spiritual beings, are fighting to protect the ecological web that sustains us all. There's a spiritual story behind this work, and it's a different story than the one commonly told by Western science, religion, and political history.

ON MAY 11, 1987, a group of hereditary chiefs of the Wet'suwet'en and Gitxsan people stood in a circle outside a courtroom in Smithers, British Columbia, and prayed. Before they entered the courtroom, the chiefs removed their carved headpieces and the blankets they wore bearing their clan crests. They took their seats wearing buttoned-up shirts and blouses and blazers. The chiefs knew they were about to compete in the white man's arena. They would have to prove their authority before a judge who was well-versed in Canadian legislation but who had little respect for their history, language, or laws.

"If we come into the court wearing our regalia and are disrespected," one chief warned, "then the shame of the disrespect will be costly to erase." Better to remove the sacred garb beforehand than risk its desecration.

The Gitxsan and Wet'suwet'en hereditary chiefs were preparing to do something that had never been attempted before: convince the Canadian legal system to acknowledge their jurisdiction over 58,000 square kilometres of land, a lushly forested river valley that their ancestors had hunted, fished, and governed since at least the last ice age.

In 1793 the first European to cross the continent by land wrote his name on a rock at the ocean's edge. Sixty-five years later the queen of England claimed the mainland of British Columbia as a colony, despite the fact that its Indigenous inhabitants outnumbered British settlers by a factor of one hundred and the Gitxsan and the Wet'suwet'en, like most of the two hundred or so First Nations who still live in what is known as British Columbia, had never signed a treaty or in any way relinquished claims to their land. Thirteen years later, in 1871, men in Ottawa signed a paper declaring the forests, rivers, and mountains the Wet'suwet'en had guarded for thousands of years part of the Dominion of

Canada. The Wet'suwet'en and Gitxsan never consented to any of this. Instead, they fought for the right to fish for salmon in their own rivers, to prevent dams from flooding their burial grounds, and to stop logging companies from clearcutting their forests. They had blockaded logging roads and railroad tracks but to little avail. Now they were taking their struggle to the courts.

The challenge they faced was that their claim to the land was inscribed in human memory but not written down on paper. "For us, the ownership of territory is a marriage of the Chief and the land," a hereditary Gitxsan chief who held the title Delgamuukw told the judge in his opening statement. "Each Chief has an ancestor who encountered and acknowledged the life of the land. From such encounters come power. The land, and plants, the animals, and the people all have spirit — they all must be shown respect. That is the basis of our law." To prove their title, they would have to open their archives, the practised memories of their chiefs and elders.

During the first four years of the trial, Gitxsan and Wet'suwet'en chiefs and elders, often working with specially trained translators, recounted oral histories, described their systems of governance, and created detailed maps showing all their clan boundaries. They recited stories, performed ceremonies, and sang songs in court to demonstrate their sacred responsibilities to the land.

Justice Allan McEachern of the Supreme Court of British Columbia listened to the case with his spectacles balanced on his nose and an expression of skeptical remove on his face. After four years of hearings, he dismissed the Gitxsan and Wet'suwet'en land claim in a nearly four-hundred-page ruling that echoed the Doctrine of Discovery. He referred to the pine-clad mountains and salmon-filled rivers of the Skeena-Bulkley valley as "a vast emptiness" and Wet'suwet'en civilization as "a much lower, even primitive order." Their oral histories, he said, had the "decided complexion of unreality" and their spiritual covenant with the land "stretche[d] credulity," he wrote. Meanwhile, he accepted without question written reports from European explorers, traders, and government officials. The Wet'suwet'en and Gitxsan had no case, McEachern said. Any land title they may have once held, he said, had been extinguished when British Columbia joined the Dominion of Canada in 1871.

The Gitxsan and the Wet'suwet'en heard the verdict and wept. Then they appealed.

Six years later, in 1997, Canada's highest court overturned McEachern's ruling. The oral histories provided by the elders and chiefs were valid in Canadian courts, the Supreme Court judges ruled. The Wet'suwet'en and Gitxsan title had never been extinguished. Due to a technical error, however, the judges said, they could not confirm that the Wet'suwet'en and Gitxsan owned the land under Canadian law. The claim remained unresolved. The case had dragged on for ten costly years. The judges advised the province and the two nations to find other means to settle their disagreements over how the land would be managed.

Finding other means to assert their sovereignty is

precisely what Freda Huson was doing in 2010 when she obtained the GPS coordinates of a planned pipeline corridor through Wet'suwet'en land and built a log cabin directly in its path on the banks of the Wedzin Kwa, a river sacred to the Wet'suwet'en people and the source of their salmon. The location was strategic. The cabin commanded a narrow wooden bridge along the only road access to an area of land governed by the clan to which Freda belongs.

Over the next decade, Freda and other Wet'suwet'en leaders evicted surveyors attempting to explore routes for pipelines and sites for mines on Wet'suwet'en territory. They established a checkpoint at the bridge and, following Wet'suwet'en law and the principles of Free, Prior and Informed Consent, anyone entering the territory had to obtain permission from hereditary leaders.

But one company wouldn't take no for an answer. In 2012 Coastal Gaslink began planning a route for a 670-kilometre pipeline with the capacity to deliver 2.1 billion cubic feet per day of natural gas to a facility on the coast at Kitimat for export to global markets. The pipeline would cross through the territories of nine house groups belonging to all five Wet'suwet'en clans. Coastal Gaslink signed agreements with twenty First Nations adjacent to the pipeline route, including some Wet'suwet'en elected band councils. But they did not get permission from the Wet'suwet'en hereditary chiefs. When Canada created the Indian Act in 1876, the Canadian government informed the Wet'suwet'en they were wards of the state and would be governed through a colonial system of elected chiefs and councils rather than their traditional leaders. But the Wet'suwet'en's traditional system of hereditary chiefs never went away. The two forms of government continued side by side. The hereditary chiefs' jurisdiction extends beyond the reserve boundaries. That was the land the pipeline would cross. In 2018 hereditary chiefs and representatives of all five of the Wet'suwet'en clans gathered in their traditional feast hall and decided to block the pipeline.

The conflict escalated. In late 2018 Coastal Gaslink asked the British Columbia courts for an injunction to remove Wet'suwet'en land defenders who had barricaded the road and were preventing them from accessing the territory. A temporary injunction was eventually granted. A few months later, police armed with military weapons rushed a blockade and arrested fourteen people.

Coastal Gaslink set up a work camp on Wet'suwet'en land. Workers and heavy machinery began to pour in. In early 2020 Freda drove up to the work camp and delivered an eviction notice signed by the hereditary chiefs ordering Coastal Gaslink to vacate the land immediately. Coastal Gaslink evacuated its employees and notified the police. Freda barricaded the bridge to prevent them from coming back. Soon, reports reached her that hotels in nearby Houston and Smithers were filling up with RCMP preparing for a major invasion.

On February 10, 2020, two days after Freda burned the injunction, the RCMP returned, this time with tactical units armed with rifles and dogs. The funeral pyre for Canada that the Wet'suwet'en matriarchs had lit at the end of the bridge was still burning. A convoy of police vehicles parked at one end of the bridge. Helicopters dropped snipers in the forest behind the camp.

Freda and other women of her clan gathered around the sacred fire at the end of the bridge. The women took turns striking a silver bell that hung from a tripod of pine poles. They called upon their ancestors to help them in their fight. They cried out the names of Indigenous women who had gone missing from their communities under the diverted gaze of local police, some in years past and many more since the arrival of industrial man camps. Red dresses hung along the bridge in memory of the women fluttered in the wind.

"You are trying to invade our land so that CGL can pollute our waters and destroy any future we have to be Wet'suwet'en," shouted Karla Tait, Freda's niece, as armed officers closed in on the small knot of women drumming and singing. "My five-year-old daughter depends on these lands to live."

As the women continued to sing, the RCMP officers dismantled the barricade across the bridge, chainsawing through the word "reconciliation" painted on it, and led the women one by one to waiting police vehicles. Freda was the last to be taken. She continued her defiant drumming and singing, her voice growing hoarse and cracking under its emotional strain, until she was driven away in a police vehicle.

THAT NIGHT IN WINNIPEG furious crowds boiled into three major intersections at the height of rush hour, carrying signs and banners that read "Wet'suwet'en Strong" and "Indigenous Sovereignty Is Climate Action." Sadie-Phoenix Lavoie, a two-spirit Anishinaabe organizer, held up an eagle feather as she led the group that seized the intersection at Portage and Main. Angry motorists, held back by police cars with flashing lights, leaned on their horns. I held the mittened hands of two strangers as we danced in a circle around the intersection. I could feel the waves of emotion flowing off the crowd. Solidarity actions had sprung up from coast to coast. Around the country people impeded traffic and commuter trains to express their anger. Mohawk warriors in Tyendinaga, Ontario, blocked railroad tracks for three weeks, preventing the transportation of goods across the country. A group of Indigenous youth took sleeping bags to the office of Dan Vandal, then Canada's minister of northern affairs, and refused to leave for ten days, demanding that RCMP get off Wet'suwet'en land. Across Canada, non-Indigenous people joined the protests. The Wet'suwet'en people's decades-old struggle had become a proxy war in our planet's struggle for survival. The Wet'suwet'en were fighting for us all.

Then the pandemic struck. The streets emptied out. Coronavirus crushed climate activism more effectively than any police enforcement could. Freda and the other women who had been arrested were released without charges, but by then the news cycle had moved on to a new global emergency. All the momentum the climate movement had built in 2019 and early 2020 appeared to fizzle.

One thing that did not stop during the pandemic

was the construction of new fossil fuel pipelines. While Wet'suwet'en communities were burying and mourning elders taken by COVID-19, Coastal Gaslink continued to work. By February 2021, 140 kilometres of the 670-kilometre pipeline was in the ground.

In June 2021, once I had my first COVID-19 vaccine, I made a trip to Wet'suwet'en territory together with four other people. The delegation was organized by Community Peacemaker Teams, an interfaith organization that provides nonviolent accompaniment and support for communities around the world facing violence and oppression. For four weeks we lived at the Unist'ot'en Healing Centre, chopping wood, caulking cabins, and building racks for smoking salmon and moose. What had started out as Freda's log cabin had become a place of cultural and political renewal for the Wet'suwet'en people. The buildings next to the waters of the Wedzin Kwa had lodging for elders, a kitchen and dining room area, and various sites for ceremony and cultural practices. Almost every weekend during our stay a vanload of Wet'suwet'en children arrived for several days of teaching from elders and ceremony on the land.

Freda Huson showed us the right-of-way that Coastal Gaslink had sheared through the forest to make way for the pipeline. A swath of forest where her people had gathered soap berries and hunted moose and performed ceremony was now a gash of splintered trees and pulverized earth 100 metres wide, stretching as far as the eye could see in either direction. It made the land defenders weep just to see it. They vowed the pipeline would never be completed.

We knew the Wet'suwet'en leaders were making plans behind the scenes for the next stage of the resistance, but we didn't know when it would happen or what it would look like.

The moment arrived at the end of September 2021. Molly Wickham, a leader from the Gidimt'en (Grizzly) clan who went by her Wet'suwet'en name Sleydo, and a small group of land defenders seized a site that Coastal Gaslink had cleared next to the river as a drill pad from which they planned to bore under the sacred headwaters of the Wedzin Kwa. Working swiftly under cover of night, Sleydo and her land defenders moved a tiny house trailer equipped with bunks and a woodstove onto a hill over-looking the muddy field Coastal Gaslink had carved out of the forest. An environmental report had recently revealed Coastal Gaslink had allowed pollutants to flow into nearby rivers and streams. The Wet'suwet'en feared for their river.

The land defenders barricaded the narrow road leading to the site with a pile of logs, a wrecked car, and an old school bus. Sleydo put out a call for support. "We want you to come here now," she said in a video posted to social media, her eyes hard as flint, one arm locked to an exca-vator. "We need legal observers, we need support on the ground. This is the fight of our lives. We have so much at stake here. Drilling under Wedzin Kwa would absolutely devastate everything that is important to us. Please come!"

Watching the video I felt a sharp pain in my chest. I knew I had to go. I'd just finished reading a report about the amount of carbon pollution Indigenous resistance had kept out of the atmosphere. I was busy writing about Indigenous communities on the front lines of the climate crisis, but it wasn't enough just to write. I needed to do more. If I believed what I was writing about, then I needed to answer Sleydo's call.

"I think I should go," I said to Mona at the breakfast table the next morning. "I'd be gone for a week. Ten days max." My mouth was dry. I couldn't swallow my oatmeal. This was very sudden, and I expected Mona to have misgivings. She knew that by setting foot in the camp I'd be violating a court injunction, putting myself at risk of arrest.

But Mona was immediately supportive. "Is this something your soul is calling you to do?" she asked.

"I think so," I said.

"Then you should go," she said. "I'll flex my work time so I can drop the kids off at school and pick them up."

By end of day, I'd rented a car and cancelled my appointments for the week. I felt like I'd crawled into someone else's skin. I'm a cautious person by nature. I like to make plans far in advance and carefully consider the risks. I was about to step into the kind of conflict I'd never navigated before.

The night before my departure I lay in bed, wracked with anxiety, second-guessing myself. Mona held me.

"I love you," I whispered.

"Then go and do this with love," she whispered back.

It was still dark the next morning when I hugged my daughter's small warm body curled in her nest of blankets and whispered, "I'll be back soon." My chest hurt. The night before, when she'd heard I was leaving, she'd clamped her knees around my leg and glared at me: "You're not going!"

I drove west as the sun crept up under a woolly cloud bank and cast its slanting orange glow across the stubbled wheat fields. Soon I was crossing Saskatchewan's gentle folded pastureland, scorched a dull brown by a summer of extreme drought. On the radio I heard beer prices were going up due to a shortage of barley. By the time I reached Regina, the temperature was nearing 30 degrees Celsius, unheard of for late September. Tears kept gathering in the corners of my eyes and tracking down my cheeks as I passed swells of desiccated pastureland. Fear ballooned in my chest. To keep myself from thinking of reasons to turn around and go back home, I kept repeating: "This is a hard thing. And you are doing it." I thought of Tara Houska, an Anishinaabe land defender from Couchouching First Nation, who had led a campaign of civil disobedience in Minnesota months earlier in a last-ditch attempt to try to stop a pipeline expansion that would carry diluted bitumen from the Alberta tar sands to a terminal on Lake Superior. After being shot with rubber bullets, burned with pepper spray, and being locked in solitary confinement, she'd sent a message to her supporters. "Pray for us. Stand with us, if you can. Find your bravery. Our Mother needs us so badly."

I didn't know whether I was following a call from God or the universe or Mother Earth, but I knew it was real. "Find your bravery," I whispered to myself as I drove.

That night I called Mona from my room in Edmonton. "I've never experienced anxiety in my body like this," I told her. I knew she'd dealt with bouts of anxiety and depression over the years. "How do you manage it?" She guided me through an exercise of putting my hand on my belly and paying attention to my breath. The ritual seemed to calm the static in my body.

What I was doing didn't have to be perfect, I reminded myself. I didn't need to know whether this campaign would succeed; it was enough to answer a call. I could trust the larger forces for good at work in the world. It helped to remember that my responsibility was to the small task before me.

I ARRIVED IN HOUSTON, a small industry town in northern British Columbia, late the next night, exhausted. I'd been on the road for fifteen hours, the last few spent hunched over my steering wheel squinting through pummelling rain and the blinding headlights of jacked-up pickup trucks. I spent the night at a house for supporters of the Wet'suwet'en land defenders. A young Gitxsan woman showed me to my room. She'd be up early in the morning, she said, driving around town, counting the vehicles at the RCMP station and local motels to see if the cops were bringing in reinforcements for a raid.

I headed out at first light the next morning, driving down muddy logging roads. On the outskirts of Houston I passed the chain-link fence behind which pipes were stacked. They slid past my window as I drove, row upon gleaming row. They seemed to go on forever.

Only days earlier, RCMP had brutalized a land defender who had locked himself to the underside of an old school bus positioned across the road. Rather than using specialized extraction equipment, police had spent an hour inflicting physical and psychological pain on the man. The video footage posted on social media was hard to watch. The man screamed as police took turns yanking on his legs. They pulled down his pants and ordered him to release himself. Finally, a mechanic was brought in to dismantle the bus so the locking mechanism could be released. The man had been arrested and taken to a hospital in Houston to have his injuries examined.

The blockade was holding, but just barely. A handful of activists, responding to Sleydo's call, had driven up from Vancouver Island, where they'd been part of an ongoing campaign to protect some of Canada's most ancient old growth forest from being cut down. They brought with them tactics that had worked well at Fairy Creek to delay logging efforts for over a year.

It was September 30, Canada's first official Day of Truth and Reconciliation. Earlier that summer, several First Nations had uncovered the unmarked graves of hundreds of Indigenous children who had died at residential schools. The findings had unleashing torrents of grief in Indigenous communities and a national reckoning for Canadians. I'd heard there was a ceremony and a feast planned at the resistance camp. Everyone was hoping the cops would stay away, for that day at least.

As I navigated the muddy logging roads, I passed a few

white pickups with Coastal Gaslink logos. All their occupants were wearing orange T-shirts. I cringed: the orange T-shirt was a symbol of solidarity with residential school survivors. This was how Canada acknowledged its history of colonization, I thought, by dressing its agents of dispossession in sympathetic orange.

I turned off the main logging road and crept up a deeply rutted spur road that led to the camp. Long-needled trees walled me in, lodgepole pines and subalpine firs and white spruces interspersed with the flaming fall orange of balsam poplars. I stopped when I reached a jumble of logs and a school bus blocking the road. An upside-down Canada flag stained with red handprints covered its grille and an orange banner hung from a log thrust crosswise through the bus's windows read: "You stole the children from the land. Wedzin Kwa belongs to the children." On the road behind the bus, a few young people in knitted sweaters and hiking boots were constructing a cage of logs with a space inside for a land defender to lock down. I guessed they were the crew from Fairy Creek.

I got out of my car and hiked past the bus and up a short hill where I found the camp headquarters built on a clearing intended for a helipad. Now it was occupied by a homemade house trailer with a pitched roof pierced by a stovepipe. Next to it a tarp sheltered a makeshift kitchen. Two immobilized yellow excavators sat idle at the edge of the camp, their cockpits draped in Mohawk warrior flags.

Sleydo, in green rubber boots and a camouflage jacket, was standing next to a campfire drinking coffee from a tin mug. I recognized her from the video. "Welcome to Coyote Camp," she said. "Want some coffee?" I introduced myself and she rounded up a few other newcomers for a quick orientation around the fire.

"This is the Cas Yikh territory, Grizzly House," Sleydo said to us. "The highest authority on this land is Dinï ze' Woos, hereditary chief of the Gidimt'en Clan of the Wet'suwet'en nation. Decisions about this camp and our strategy are made by our hereditary leadership. I answer to our leaders, and they answer to the Wet'suwet'en people. You are guests on Wet'suwet'en land. Welcome." She bent down and picked up a piece of charcoal from the fire.

"Our ancestors are here fighting with us," Sleydo said. "They may not recognize you as friends." She stepped toward me and performed a ceremonial gesture with the charcoal. "This will help the ancestors recognize you," she said. "On this territory you'll be safe."

As we stood around the fire, elders and chiefs and families with children came streaming up the hill carrying boxes of sandwiches, crockpots full of chili, and trays of brownies for the feast. It had been raining for weeks, but now the clouds peeled away and blue sky appeared over Coyote Camp. The atmosphere turned festive: lawn chairs were unfolded around the fire, children climbed on the excavators like jungle gyms.

The hereditary chiefs donned their formal regalia — carved headpieces and crested blankets. Drummers led a procession that circled the fire where representatives from the five Wet'suwet'en clans took turns speaking. Dinï ze'

Smogelgem, a tall man with a fringed black-and-yellow blanket draped over his shoulders, hereditary chief of the Likhts'amisyi (Fireweed) Clan, spoke of the trauma of residential schools: "We still live with that pain. We still live with that trauma. Every time we breathe, every time we move, we're reminded of the pain of our people."

Dinï ze' Namoks, hereditary chief of the Tsayu (Beaver) Clan, reminded us that the spirits of the children who had died at residential schools were gathered with us today. He asked for two minutes and fifteen seconds of silence in memory of the two hundred and fifteen graves found at the Kamloops Residential School. Two hundred fifteen children who had been taken from their families and never returned. I thought of my own children and felt a tightness in my throat. We stood in silence. A raven circling overhead uttered a low croak. Wind moved over the shorn hilltop. I could see the path for the pipeline razored through the forest, a brutal scar on the land.

After the silence we each put a pinch of tobacco in the fire to honour the children. Sleydo and another woman drummed and sang a mourning song for the children and for the land, their voices braiding together, sweet and sorrowful.

"We have children to protect still," said Sleydo when her song was finished, her eyes like chips of glass. "When the Indian agents came with the RCMP to remove children from their home territory, we couldn't do anything. But we can do something now!" As she spoke, one of her daughters, a toddler, who had been playing in a mud puddle, raised her arms to her mother and started to cry. Sleydo's partner, Cody, picked her up, but the girl cried harder and stretched her mud-covered arms toward her mother. Sleydo shrugged off the ankle-length fur coat she was wearing and handed it to her sister so it wouldn't get dirty, then took her muddy daughter and cradled the girl on her hip as she continued to speak.

"We are a powerful people. The Wet'suwet'en people have always been a powerful people. Along with our Gitxsan allies, we stood together for thousands of years to protect our territories. We are doing the same thing now, to defend our land for our children so they never have to experience what the children from residential schools experienced."

MY JOB DURING THE week I spent in Wet'suwet'en territory was to sit at the end of the spur road leading up to Coyote Camp in a pickup truck with a CB radio and report the movements of police vehicles on the main logging road. Each morning I woke up at 4:30 in the shivering darkness, gathered bannock, fruit, teabags, and coffee from the kitchen tent, and drove to the end of the road. I was part of a network of observers with radios who provided an early warning system for the camp, giving people time to get into position if the police showed up for a raid.

I wasn't the only one watching the road. A truck marked with the logo of Forsythe Security, a private surveillance company hired by Coastal Gaslink, sat metres away from me. The driver, a red-faced man with a white goatee and a ballcap, kept his truck idling all day and a dash-mounted video camera pointed at me.

Each morning I positioned my truck so it blocked the security guard's view of me, kindled a fire to keep warm, and brewed myself a pot of coffee while keeping an ear open for the crackle of my radio.

A raven visited me every day while I kept watch. Sleydo had pointed out a raven near Coyote Camp that she said had warned them the first time the police showed up. I wondered if this was the same one. The raven announced itself each time it flew over, and I soon learned to identify a few of its many signals: a single capped note like a drop of water falling into a well, a cascade of gurgles like wine in a bottle's throat.

The anxiety I'd experienced on the drive up gradually subsided. But I never lost the uncomfortable feeling that I'd had stepped over a line that put me on the other side of the law. The RCMP, Coastal Gaslink, and Forsythe Security were all working together. Security guards and the RCMP who drove by daily marked my every move. This was a new experience for me. This was what the Wet'suwet'en lived with every day. On their own land.

The RCMP visited the camp several times during the week I was there, but they made no more arrests. They came in groups of six or eight and examined the log barricades, checked on the machinery, and dropped casual threats of violence. One officer emptied a cistern full of drinking water with a smirk on his face. We knew they were getting ready for something. Helicopters circled the camp.

The threat of police violence contrasted jarringly with the quiet beauty of the land. I gathered poplar leaves from the road, sharp as blades, bright as beaten gold, wide as my palm. I set them on the dashboard of my truck and pressed them in the pages of the novel I was reading. Later at home I opened the book to find they had all faded to a disappointing parchment brown. I'd wanted to capture something of the beauty of the place, but its majesty could not be preserved in the pages of a book.

One afternoon two young women wearing denim jackets and silver-and-turquoise rings pulled up to ask me directions to Coyote Camp. They were from a nation that neighboured the Wet'suwet'en and had come to see the camp and deliver supplies. On their way back out a few hours later, they stopped to thank me. Overhead, the raven dropped a note into the air and one of the women said: "She can feel the love." Another vehicle pulled up. It was Sleydo's sister, Jen Wickham. She got out of her car and the three women stood together in the middle of the road, smoking and talking, their late afternoon shadows stretching to the trees. One of the women mentioned a historical photo she'd seen that showed thousands of her ancestors assembled for a potlatch, a ceremony the government outlawed from 1885 until 1951. "Tens of thousands of us," she said. She waved her cigarette in a sweeping arc. "Now how many are we? A few hundred. We're survivors. It's a miracle we're even here."

As they were speaking, two white Forsythe Security trucks pulled up. The women ignored them, standing in the middle of the road, blocking their way. They talked and laughed and flicked ash from their cigarettes until the Forsythe trucks turned around and drove away.

WHAT DOES THE END of the world look like when you've already experienced it? During the nineteenth and early twentieth centuries, smallpox, influenza, and other plagues brought by settlers wiped out 75–90 percent of the Indigenous population in the Pacific Northwest. Whole villages were buried in mass graves. Then came prospectors looking for gold. They brought with them guns, alcohol, and prostitution. Wet'suwet'en women were fed alcohol and raped. Missionaries worked to snuff out Wet'suwet'en beliefs. Some people who resisted were publicly whipped and locked in wooden boxes. Priests shamed Wet'suwet'en women for having children out of wedlock. The patriarchal society of the settlers saw the matrilineal authority of Wet'suwet'en women as a threat. They sought to undermine it through punishment and shame. Indian agents seized Wet'suwet'en children and took them to residential schools. Government officials outlawed feast halls and burned the regalia of hereditary chiefs. The federal government tried to weaken the traditional governance systems by establishing the Indian Act and announcing their intention to deal only with the elected chiefs and band councils. Settlers pulled salmon from the rivers while Wet'suwet'en people were forbidden to sell fish themselves. Logging companies took the trees. The climate crisis has revealed to many of us the ways that colonial dominion and capitalist extraction are destroying the earth. But the Wet'suwet'en already know it. They have known it for a very long time.

Vine Deloria Jr., the late Sioux intellectual whose politics and theology influenced a generation of politically active Indigenous people, once described Christianity as a religion divorced from place and obsessed with time. The Apostle Paul's great innovation, he wrote, was to disconnect the faith from a particular people and their land and recast it as a universal religion, a claim that has carried Christian missionaries to every continent and has been used by European sovereigns to justify the seizure of lands belonging to non-Christians. Indigenous spiritualities, by contrast, are anchored to the land, Deloria wrote. Their mountains and hills and rivers and forests hold stories and revelations. You can't move Wet'suwet'en spirituality from its geography any more than you can move the Wedzin Kwa to Mongolia.

This is what's at stake in this pipeline fight. It's more than a forest or a river. It's a people, a culture, a spiritual relationship with the land that goes back thousands of years. What happens to that relationship when the mountains are blasted to make way for a pipeline or a river dries up because of climate change? It cannot be permitted.

Christianity is inseparable from the Western idea of history; both advance along a linear timeline toward a climax of conquest, Deloria wrote. But for the Wet'suwet'en and other Indigenous Peoples, time doesn't have the same controlling power. The apocalypse has come and is always coming. The people are still here. Their time is not a universal value; it is "a time internal to the complex relationships themselves."

If time can bend, then the end of the world is also its beginning. Many Indigenous nations speak of a prophecy — the Anishinaabe call it the Eighth Fire — that after seven generations of suffering at the hands of the colonial system, Indigenous Peoples will reclaim their traditions, their culture, their land. The climate crisis has brought together Indigenous land defenders and water protectors supporting each other in sister struggles across the continent — from Beaver Lake Cree fighting against the expansion of Alberta's massive oil sands, to the Tsleil-Waututh on the coast of British Columbia opposing the Trans Mountain Pipeline expansion, to the Gwich'in of Alaska creating a caribou refuge on their coastal plains where oil and gas development is banned. These struggles have created new opportunities for pan-Indigenous solidarity around the globe. At Standing Rock in 2016, more than three hundred Indigenous nations raised their flags.

MY WEEK AT COYOTE Camp came to an end. At the end of my last shift, I drove up the road to say my farewells. A flurry of tiny wet snowflakes swirled in the beam of my headlights. I parked the truck at a barricade and hiked up the hill to the camp. Sleydo and another supporter were tending the fire. I could hear chainsaws buzzing in the forest. New defences were being built. During my stay, the camp had been transformed from a few structures and a handful of people into a well-populated citadel guarded by a log barricade. A log cabin and a teepee had been erected in a field Coastal Gaslink had cleared. Word of the resistance was spreading and more supporters were arriving every day.

Sleydo and Freda were two different strategists fighting the same war, I thought. Freda, the master of ceremonies, had orchestrated a visual pageant that revealed colonial violence for all of Canada to see. Sleydo, the tactician, was incorporating a more militant array of strategies to draw out the resistance as long as she could.

Sleydo thanked me for my work and sent her gratitude to Mona for taking care of the household and our children so I could be out on the land. She spoke wistfully of her own family, of lying on the trampoline with her children watching a meteor shower. As she knelt to retrieve her tin coffee mug from a rock where it had been warming near the fire, the glow of the flames flickered on her camouflage jacket and fur hat. I had an image of a nurturing parent and a resolute warrior. She knew the struggle for her people's land would not be over in her lifetime. Whether or not the pipeline went through, she had inherited this fight from her ancestors and she would pass it on to her children.

Six weeks later, Sleydo and other land defenders were sitting around a fire singing, drumming, preparing mentally and spiritually for the raid they knew was coming. In the weeks after I left, the conflict escalated. Hereditary chiefs once again issued an eviction notice to Coastal Gaslink, only this time the workers didn't leave. After giving them eight hours to evacuate, land defenders cut off the logging roads to the camp. At the fireside, Sleydo had just heard that a charter plane full of RCMP had arrived in the nearby town of Smithers. With the orange firelight on her face, she told a story about a Wet'suwet'en man living in Vancouver's Downtown Eastside, strung out on alcohol and drugs. He'd heard about the Wet'suwet'en resistance and, for the first time in his life, felt proud to be Wet'suwet'en. He stopped using substances. "So remember all of the people ... that will be affected by this," Sleydo said, looking at the land defenders gathered around the fire, "all the people that will be proud to be Native people because of the stance we are taking. That has always stayed with me during every fight, during every conflict, during all the shit and all the risk and all the sacrifices ... The aftermath of what's going to happen is that people will be inspired all over the world by the contributions that you've all made here ... It will be remembered forever. And that is going to inspire people to keep fighting."

The following day, RCMP descended on Wet'suwet'en territory with assault rifles, dogs, helicopters, and drones. It was fifty-six days since Sleydo had occupied the drill site on the banks of the Wedzin Kwa. RCMP armed in military gear axed open the door to Sleydo's cabin, pointed assault rifles at her and her companions, and escorted them all to jail, along with elders, journalists, and Gitxsan, Haida, and Haudenosaunee allies. Then they burned Coyote Camp to the ground.

ON MY DRIVE UP to Wet'suwet'en territory I had listened to a CBC interview with Andrew Potter, a Canadian journalist and professor whose book *On Decline* argues that Western civilization has reached its peak and has entered a period of decline. Growth has stagnated. Social media and reactionary politics are undermining liberal democracy. We are losing the ability to deal with increasingly dire problems, ecological breakdown not least among them. Later, I'd lain awake thinking about Potter's prognostication. I didn't disagree with anything he'd said, but it felt like something was missing. It was during my long drive home that I realized what it was. There'd been no mention of the spiritual in his analysis, that dimension of human experience from which our deepest stories emanate.

We in the West are witnessing the unravelling of a story, a story of unhindered progress and divine favour and technological ascendency and human achievement. This was the story European settlers told themselves when they perceived an empty land given to them by God. This was the story Justice McEachern referenced when he called the pine-clad mountains and salmon-filled rivers of the Wet'suwet'en "a vast emptiness."

That is the story that is ending. Another story is taking its place.

Different lands have different gods, Deloria wrote. Deloria died in 2005, but he believed that Indigenous Peoples would soon rise to reclaim their heritage and their lands: "That is when the invaders of the North American continent will finally discover that for this land, god is red."

As I drove home and watched the great jagged mountains tumble into the long soft sweep of the prairies, I tried to imagine what it would look like for me to honour the god of this land. Was it too late for Christianity to give up its claims of universal truth, to acknowledge other gods? Such a work of unravelling and repenting would surely involve erasing property lines and returning land. It would mean grasping the two ends of its timeline — creation and apocalypse — and bending them so they joined. It might involve fracturing a universal religion into many small non-exclusive faiths, each in deep relationship with the land. For many of us it would mean leaving the warm comfort of our houses and showing up at places like Coyote Camp.

During my time at the Unist'ot'en Healing Centre, I'd gotten to know Freda's aunt, Doris Rosso, a stern-faced elder with a halo of curly white hair who chain-smoked and swore at the Coastal Gaslink trucks whenever they sped through the camp. She knew the name of every plant on the land. One day, she took me down to the Wedzin Kwa and told me to hold out my hands and feel its energy. "Does the river have a spirit?" I asked. "Of course," she said. She often prayed aloud in her language. When she prayed, she addressed her prayers to "Sizi Clee," Jesus Christ in Wet'suwet'en. Indigenous spiritualities have never claimed universal truth. For this reason, says Deloria, they have been able to incorporate images, stories, and rituals from other religions. In places where elements of Christianity have taken root within Indigenous culture, it has been because Christianity has adopted the outlook of the people of the land.

One evening at dinner Doris bowed her head and prayed in English so we would all understand. At the end of her prayer, she asked Sizi Clee to make Coastal Gaslink go "broke, broke, broke." She paused, and then spelled it out: "B-R-O-K-E." When she opened her eyes and looked around, she had a mischievous glint in her pupils. "Sometimes you just have to spell it out for him," she said.

Chapter 7

DISOBEDIENT

I WANT TO KNOW how to pray. It's December 2021. Advent. A season of waiting. Everything is waiting. Waiting for the pandemic to be over. Waiting for our leaders to start acting like we're in a climate emergency. Waiting for our hemisphere to tilt back into the light. We are hunkered down for our second COVID Christmas, separated from what we need most: each other.

Meanwhile, in British Columbia, the City of Abbotsford is under water. The town of Merritt has been evacuated. Fifteen thousand people across British Columbia have fled their homes. Six hundred twenty-eight thousand chickens have drowned. Four hundred twenty dairy cows and twelve thousand pigs are dead. One hundred ten beehives are swamped. Mere months ago a heat wave killed more than six hundred humans and cooked a billion sea creatures. Then came the wildfires that incinerated towns and turned forests into thickets of blackened pencils and baked spongy soils into hardened surfaces that now funnel the rain in torrents.

Heat, fire, and flood. Climate calamities come in threes now. And still our leaders bicker over diluted promises, unlikely to be kept and wholly inadequate for the emergency at hand. And still our government finds the resources to send a plane full of RCMP to invade Wet'suwet'en territory and arrest land defenders blocking a fossil fuel pipeline. On the day Sleydo is arrested, I join a handful of friends who carry banners to the RCMP headquarters in Winnipeg. We block traffic for an hour and a half in a bitter wind. Truckers curse us. A bus driver mutters to his passengers that he wishes he could run us down, his words later reported to me by a friend who happened to be on the bus.

Back at home I warm up with a bowl of soup. I read an op-ed in the *National Post* by a group of Wet'suwet'en people who disagree with the land defenders. "Militant actions" are not the Wet'suwet'en way, they say. They want outsiders like me to stay out of their affairs. Suddenly my energy is gone. I'm deflated, like an inner tube gone slack, floored by a wave of doubt. If I can have only one thing, I want it to be the assurance that I am doing the right thing. If the world crumbles, I want to know that at least I did what I was called to do. Now, even that small certainty seems out of reach.

I need a light, something to guide me. I ask Ulla for a practice or a teaching. Something to help me when despair washes over me at unexpected moments. Look for Spirit, Ulla reminds me. "There's a mystery bigger than we can know with our human senses. You're part of that mystery, I fully believe that." She tells me to walk in the forest. Read a poem. Light a candle. Keep trying. It takes work. There are no shortcuts.

Mona and I hang a star in our window. We tramp a spiral in the snow in our front yard and walk the labyrinth with our children, placing candles in jars on stumps as we sing: "Hope before us, hope behind us, hope under our feet." Our neighbour comes out to smoke on his front porch and watches our ritual with puzzled amusement. "I know you got your whole environmental thing going on," he says, leaning over the fence. "You should try sprinkling diesel fuel around your foundation. Keeps the mice from getting in. Old farm trick."

We go cross-country skiing in the forest. Our daughter cries because her hands are cold, and I offer her pieces of gingerbread to keep her moving until she warms up. I watch her struggle up a hill between shaggy spruces, her snow-suited legs soldiering on. The sun lays bars of smoke blue and lemon yellow across our path. My chest hurts with love for her and for the bewitching, fragile world she inhabits. We're still here, I tell myself. We're alive. The earth is alive. I cannot let myself forget it. Hope before us, hope behind us, hope under our feet.

I watch a video on YouTube, footage from an event live-streamed almost two years ago, on February 4, 2019. Four Catholic activists trudge through knee-deep snow toward a fenced-in valve shut-off site along the Line 3 pipeline that runs parallel to the highway about 80 kilometres west of

Duluth. They carry a pair of bolt cutters and an orange Home Depot bucket full of rosaries, prayer flags, tobacco ties, and other sacred objects people have sent them from all over the country. They snip the padlock on the fence, enter the valve site, and attempt to shut off the flow of oil, but they are missing the right size of Allen wrench to turn a screw that will give them access to the valve. They try to fashion a tool from a tiny metal crucifix, asking Christ for forgiveness as they remove his tiny suffering body from the metal cross. They hang rosaries on the fence and on the pipe itself. They call on saints to help them, saints who also broke the law for the greater good: Franz Jägerstätter, executed in 1943 for refusing to join the Nazi army, and Philip Berrigan, arrested more than one hundred times for acts of civil disobedience protesting nuclear weapons.

As I watch these four strangers fumble with inadequate tools and faltering faith, something ignites in me. These disobedient saints are swimming in a current I cannot see but can surely feel. Their wavering voices join together in a hymn. It's a song I've heard before but only in church. Here at the scene of a crime against the powers of fossil fuel capitalism, the words have a new meaning:

> From the halls of power to the fortress tower, not a
> stone will be left on stone.
> Let the king beware for your justice tears every tyrant
> from his throne.
> The hungry poor shall weep no more for the food they
> can never earn.

There are tables spread, every mouth be fed, for the
world is about to turn.

Could the world be about to turn? The song brings
tears to my eyes. The melody is an old Irish folk tune, the
words adapted from a song attributed to Mary, the mother
of Jesus. Single, pregnant, poor, a member of an occupied
people, she has just learned her child will defy an empire.
She doesn't know it will cost him his life. Through my
computer speakers I can hear the police sirens coming.

THE TIME FOR DISOBEDIENCE is now.

Only a nonviolent rebellion can save us, wrote Roger
Hallam in a manifesto he self-published in 2019. A year
earlier, thousands of activists — many with no previous
experience of public protest — had simultaneously blockaded five bridges across the Thames River, gridlocking central
London. They called themselves Extinction Rebellion and
waved banners bearing the logo of an emptying hourglass.
Hallam, an organic farmer with a beaklike nose, a scraggly
grey ponytail, and fierce deep-set eyes, had spent the last
decade studying civil resistance movements. He helped
launch Extinction Rebellion because he believed a popular
uprising was the only thing that would make governments
act on the climate emergency. Thousands of Londoners were
arrested, overwhelming the courts and clogging the jails, a
strategy reminiscent of civil rights activists in the 1960s.
By the spring of 2019, after months of public disruption,

the British Parliament agreed to declare a climate emergency. Farhana Yamin, an environmental lawyer who helped draft the Paris Agreement, told the *Guardian* she joined Extinction Rebellion because she was fed up with the egos and denialism holding back real change. She'd left the world of international diplomacy and had found a lever she could move, out on the streets. Veteran climate activist Bill McKibben has called nonviolent direct action "the greatest technology invented in the twentieth century" and our best hope in the climate struggle.

In 2019 I too began to pin my hopes on the power of disruptive mass movements. I'd been reading some of the latest research into the efficacy of nonviolent civil resistance. In 2011 Erica Chenoweth, a thirty-one-year-old scholar in the field of international relations, published a paper that caught the world's attention. Initially skeptical of the claims made about nonviolent resistance, Chenoweth and their colleague Maria Stephan had spent two years cataloguing every civil uprising, revolution, and armed insurrection from the past century. They found, to their astonishment, that nonviolent uprisings achieved their goals nearly twice as often as violent ones. What's more, the research showed that "the active and sustained participation of just 3.5 percent of the population" was enough to topple a regime or win democratic reforms. The 3.5 percent rule, as it came to be known, was seized by climate organizers everywhere.

Organizing for social change is often slow, painstaking work, but sometimes the dominoes fall with lightning speed. A repressive regime firmly in power on Monday is toppled on Tuesday. A long-held societal injustice — laws against same-sex marriage, for instance — crumbles seemingly overnight. Victories like these are usually the fruit of years of behind-the-scenes organizing. But they give climate organizers hope.

In the summer of 2019 I had joined a crowd of concerned people gathered in the common room of the University of Winnipeg. Later, we would organize formally under the name Manitoba Energy Justice Coalition, but at the time we were merely a group of people who had come together because we wanted to do something about the climate crisis. We spent that summer organizing one of the largest mass protests in Winnipeg's history. When twelve thousand people circled the Manitoba Legislature on September 26, demanding action on climate change, it felt like the movement was just starting to gain momentum. Then the pandemic hit.

Two years later, on a rainy evening in September 2021, I found myself sitting masked in a carefully spaced circle in the airy sanctuary of a United Church. This was a different kind of group. Around the circle were Anglicans, Quakers, Mennonites, and a few people who didn't identify with a religious tradition but were interested participating in spiritual civil disobedience. Our target was TD Bank, one of the largest financiers of the tar sands, and a principal lender to the Line 3 expansion project scheduled for completion in Minnesota that fall. The Canadian part of the project was done, but on the other side of the border, Anishinaabe land defenders were fighting to stop the pipeline from being built across their treaty lands.

I'd never participated in a religious public protest before. My family came from a branch of Mennonites who eschewed political action. They refused to serve in the military, the police force, or elected office. My parents had never voted. We were citizens of heaven, I was told, not of this world. As a child, I'd learned to use the tool of spirituality, but the tool of politics had been forbidden. As an adult, I'd put my spirituality aside and gotten involved in political organizing, but all my work had been with secular groups. (I associated religious protest with rallies against abortion or same-sex marriage.) Now I wanted to pick up my spirituality again, but I didn't know how to hold both of those tools at once.

I was interested in the question of how churches could be marshalled in the struggle for climate justice. A few, like the Wild Churches, seemed ready. But most churches were quiet. I couldn't understand how churches could be so silent about the greatest humanitarian crisis of our time. Churches seemed to have so much potential. They were influential communities, often bound together by deep religious convictions about working for the collective good and prioritizing the needs of the most vulnerable. Yet I'd been disappointed at how few churches or people of faith showed up at climate rallies. But here in this sanctuary I was seeing faces I'd never seen before at secular rallies. Could it be, I wondered, that some people needed the symbols and language of spirituality to bring them to protest?

Our group planned and executed a series of actions at three different TD branches. At one, we held an exorcism to cast out the spirit of greed; at another, we sat in a circle in the parking lot in meditative silence like a Quaker meeting. There were no chants or speeches, only our signs voiced our message. At a third branch, two Anglican priests in white gowns and green stoles served communion with silver tongs. "Learn to live not as children of colonialism, but as children of the Creator," said one of the priests. Our actions drew indignation from bank security, nervous glances from TD clients, and puzzled looks from passersby.

My feelings about the actions were complicated. I loved the deep and pregnant silence of the Quaker gathering. It was a refreshing change from the righteous cacophony of the secular rallies I usually participated in. We were bearing silent witness, listening instead of shouting. At the Anglican service I felt like more of an outsider. The 2.5-metre gilt cross, the robed priests, the silver chalice seemed like relics of an imperious faith. It felt like a form of public theatre, though I wasn't sure how well we were communicating with the public. In a way, that didn't seem to matter to others in our group: there was a sense that we were influencing reality on another plane. When we debriefed afterward, one person, a softspoken musician who identified as a Quaker, said something that intrigued me. We were talking about how to get the attention of TD executives. "We have a responsibility for their souls," he said. Later I asked him what he'd meant. Quakers, he explained, believe that there is "something of God" in every person. We had a responsibility to seek to transform the hearts of bank executives as well as curtailing their power to do harm. This work of transformation also applied to us. We had to "challenge the evil in ourselves," he said. I'd never thought of public protest as something that could change *me* as well.

When I watched the footage of the four Catholic valve turners, though, I could sense something powerful at work. Like the current of the Wedzin Kwa that Doris Rosso had invited me to reach out and feel.

IN DECEMBER 2021 I rented a car and drove south, across the U.S. border and then east to Duluth, Minnesota. I was going to visit Michele Naar-Obed, one of the four valve turners. I wanted to know what motivated a person to dedicate her life to civil disobedience the way she had, sacrificing years of her life to courtrooms and jail cells, all for the sake of change that seemed to happen painfully slowly or not at all.

It was night by the time I pulled up at a two-storey house with pale blue vinyl siding and a "Stop Line 3" sign in the front yard. Michele and I had spoken on the phone. I'd told her about my research, and she'd invited me to come visit her at Hildegard House, where she and her husband, Greg Boertje-Obed, lived together with an Anishinaabe water protector awaiting her court date and a migrant worker seeking asylum.

Michele met me at the door, brimming with energy,

her greying hair tied tightly at her nape and fanning out over her shoulders. It was late, but she invited me to join her and Greg for a cup of tea. Greg, bespectacled and bearded, greeted me softly from the couch in the living room. Greg and Michele, both in their midsixties, wore pilly fleece sweaters over plaid shirts and patched jeans, rolled at the cuffs. The house was clean and down-at-the-heels. The floors creaked, the cast-iron radiators sighed, and the plastic film glued over the windows to keep out the cold crackled in the draft.

Hildegard House was a Catholic Worker house, part of a network of autonomous communities committed to nonviolence, voluntary simplicity, prayer, and works of mercy. Catholic Workers orient themselves around Jesus's teachings about serving the poor, but they operate without the approval or oversight of the Roman Catholic Church. The first Catholic Worker house was started during the Great Depression in New York City by Dorothy Day, a journalist and anti-poverty activist. It's hard to say whom Day irritated more, the church or the government. As a young woman she had an illegal abortion, drank liberally, and hung around with Marxists. At thirty, she converted to Catholicism and started a socialist newspaper she called the *Catholic Worker*. Its first issue asked: "Is it not possible to be radical without being atheistic?" Day opened her house to the poor and destitute as though they were Christ himself. She denounced conscription at a time when the Catholic Church supported the war effort. When air-raid drill sirens commanded the public to take shelter, she organized a demonstration at city hall. Day broke any law she believed unjust and spent many a day in court and night in jail. The FBI had a file on her and debated whether she should be detained in the event of a national emergency.

Pouring myself a cup of tea in the kitchen, I saw a photo propped in a spice rack of Day at age seventy-five, sitting on a stool in a field surrounded by Cesar Chavez's striking farm workers, her wrinkled hands folded on her knees. Shot from a low angle, the photo framed her between the holstered hips of two U.S. police officers. Her lips were pursed; she was about to lecture the cops with the words of Christ: Blessed are the poor, for theirs is the kingdom of God.

I asked Michele what she thought about the Catholic Church's move to consider Day for sainthood. Michele laughed. Hers was a boisterous contagious laugh I would soon be well acquainted with. "*Now* they want to make her a saint!" she said. "When she was alive, they told her to change the name of her newspaper!" It was true. The archbishop of New York, worried that people would mistake the *Catholic Worker*'s socialist views for those of the church, told Day to change its name. She politely declined.

"The Catholic Church has already done so much damage," Michele said, shaking her head. "You'd think they'd see that the best thing they could do at this point is fold it all up. Tear up your fucking doctrines. Let the true faith come out!" There was laughter in her voice, but she was dead serious. Greg sipped his tea on the couch. His quiet energy seemed the opposite of Michele's fervour. She broke into a jog just to cross the kitchen.

Our conversation moved to Jessica Reznicek, an environmental activist who had lived for a time at Hildegard House and was now serving an eight-year prison sentence for using a welding torch to cut holes in a series of oil pipelines. When I mentioned I'd written to her in jail, Greg asked if I'd used white paper. I said I'd written on a yellow legal pad.

"They'll send it back," Greg said. It turned out he knew the prison system well. Between the two of them, he and Michele had spent a total of eight years in jail, mainly for protesting nuclear weapons. When their daughter was young, they'd tried to stagger their acts of civil disobedience so someone was always at home with her.

The path that led Michele to activism was the same one that led her to Christianity. She told me her story the next morning as the three of us drove out to the spot on the Mississippi River where she had spent her summer camping out in the path of Line 3.

Michele grew up Catholic, but the rituals of Mass — still said in Latin at the time — had little meaning for her. In January 1991 Michele was in her midthirties, working at a lab in a hospital in Baltimore. She hadn't been to church in years. That month the United States launched Operation Desert Storm, a forty-two-day aerial bombing campaign against Iraq. Angry about the war, Michele went to a Quaker-led vigil she'd read about in a community flyer. At the vigil, a group of anti-war activists invited her to join them in planning a direct action. It sounded exciting. A few weeks later, Michele and a handful of others scaled the

Armory Building in Baltimore and poured blood, sand, and oil down its side. Michele was arrested and spent a night in jail. It was her first experience of civil disobedience, and it exhilarated her.

Through the action, Michele met members of Jonah House, a community of Christian anti-war activists, among them ex-soldier, ex-priest Philip Berrigan and his wife Elizabeth McAlister, a former nun. They were leaders in a radical Christian anti-nuclear weapons movement called Plowshares, after the words of the prophet Isaiah, who envisioned a world where militaries would be disbanded and swords would be hammered into farming implements. On September 9, 1980, eight peace activists, including Philip Berrigan and his brother, Daniel Berrigan, a Jesuit priest, had walked into a weapons assembly plant in King of Prussia, Pennsylvania, and hammered on the nose cones of two nuclear warheads and poured blood on them. The Plowshares Eight, as they came to be known, were arrested and managed to turn their highly publicized trial into a referendum on nuclear proliferation. Since then, Plowshares activists have carried out hundreds of similar actions targeting nuclear weapons in the United States, England, Australia, Germany, Holland, Sweden, and Ireland.

Michele had never met Christians like these before. Plowshares activists spent months — sometimes years — preparing for actions. They studied maps of shipyards and blueprints of submarines, but they also prepared themselves emotionally and spiritually by reading Scripture, praying, and talking. "You don't know what you're facing. You've got to be grounded in something that's really deeper than you," Michele told me. She eventually moved into Jonah House after her boss at the hospital told her she couldn't keep her job if she kept getting arrested.

Michele started reading the Bible and attending liturgy with her housemates. She read Howard Zinn's *A People's History of the United States*. Suddenly the stories of Hebrew prophets living under Babylonian occupation or early Christians confronting the Roman Empire came alive for her. "It's happening right now; and we are living it!" she remembers thinking.

One overcast morning in August 1995, Michele and four others quickly snipped through a chain-link fence surrounding a shipyard in Newport News, Virginia. Wearing white hardhats and fake ID badges with barcodes cut from cereal boxes, they mingled with the shipyard workers and made their way to the docks, where they boarded a nuclear-powered fast-attack submarine, the USS *Greeneville*. They hammered on the submarine's missile launch tubes, poured out their own blood, which they'd been collecting in baby bottles, and unfurled a banner bearing a photo of a Japanese mother nursing her child, the tiny infant's face scorched by the blast of a nuclear bomb. Then, as they waited to be arrested, they knelt and began to pray.

This was the second time activists had infiltrated the Newport News facility, and the shipyard was embarrassed. The U.S. military was threatening to take its contracts elsewhere. "These are billion-dollar contracts," Michele said to me. "They would rather see you dead than lose them." Michele and her companions were hit with a slew of felony charges — trespassing, damage to property, sabotage, conspiracy — carrying a total of up to sixty years in prison and $1.2 million in fines. In the end they took a plea bargain, pleading guilty to conspiracy in exchange for the rest of their charges being dropped. A repeat offender, Michele received the longest sentence of eighteen months. She was forty-one years old with a two-year-old daughter. Michele was sent to a federal prison in Florida. Every three months Greg and their daughter made the 3,000-kilometre round trip from Baltimore to Tallahassee to visit Michele in jail.

Michele said she couldn't have survived this ordeal without two things: a spiritual grounding and a community of support.

Mohandas Gandhi developed a theory of nonviolent resistance to evil he called *satyagraha*. It involved voluntarily accepting suffering into your body in order to disarm your enemy. This is spiritual work: you must be willing to experience pain, even face death, without knowing the outcome of your actions. In the same vein, Freedom Riders in the 1960s defied American segregation laws as they rode buses deeper and deeper into the South, knowing they could be beaten, imprisoned, or even killed. Some were. Many found courage by identifying with Christ, who faced crucifixion. These were examples Michele turned to as she prepared for her actions, along with the writings of the biblical prophets.

But she needed a community to support her as well, Michele told me. She'd seen young people give everything

they had to a movement. But without a spiritual grounding or a community of support, "It destroyed them," she
said. Plowshares supporters would pack the courtroom
whenever their people were on trial. At one of Michele's
hearings — a story she recounted with considerable
delight — the courtroom was so full of cheering supporters
that the judge ordered it cleared. At another hearing, they
sang hymns until the exasperated judge ordered all of them
detained. The Plowshares community also helped take care
of Michele's family while she was serving time and was
there to celebrate when she was released. They reminded
her that she was part of something bigger than herself.

JONATHAN MATTHEW SMUCKER, A Mennonite political
organizer who helped organize the Occupy Wall Street
movement, has critiqued the Plowshares movement for
its lack of political calculus. Smucker spent two years in a
Catholic Worker community in Washington, D.C., in the
1990s. He helped organize actions and campaigns around
the war in Iraq and oil drilling in Nigeria. He was arrested
twenty times. At the Catholic Worker he found a politically
engaged, deeply spiritual community that gave him a sense
of belonging and purpose, but he questioned the long-term
effectiveness of the work. In his book *Hegemony How-To:
A Roadmap for Radicals*, Smucker wonders whether the
spiritual activism of the Plowshares movement is too
inward focused, a form of highly sacrificial, symbolic activism that strengthens its own subculture and creates a sense

of spiritual purpose but fails to build a broader social movement or achieve concrete political goals.

I asked Michele about this. She and others had endured dehumanizing incarceration, anxiety-inducing surveillance, and physical and psychological abuse by law enforcement. Collectively, Plowshares activists had spent many decades in jail. Was all of it worth it? Had anything shifted? Michele has wrestled with these questions. Her first Plowshares action didn't even delay the launch of the submarine: "A couple of dents that they sandpapered over," she said. "I remember being devastated. I felt like a complete failure." But years later, at an event commemorating the hundreds of thousands of Japanese civilians killed when the United States dropped atomic bombs on Japan, Michele heard the grandchild of one of the survivors speak. In the decades since Hiroshima and Nagasaki, he said, no nuclear weapon had been used. In that moment Michele saw her work as a tiny part of a global struggle for peace. In some immeasurable way, she believed, her actions had helped bend the moral arc of the universe.

Listening to Michele, I tried to assess the value of our symbolic actions in front of TD banks in Winnipeg. Our righteous theatre hadn't mobilized a critical mass of people in the pews or on the streets. I wondered what it would take. It seemed to me that a successful movement to pressure governments to take the necessary action on climate change would require both visible, symbolic acts of disruption like those of Plowshares, but also the more painstaking work of community organizing that Smucker advocates for.

ABOUT 80 KILOMETRES SOUTH of Grand Rapids, Michele, Greg, and I pulled over and parked on the shoulder. A swath had been cut through a mixed forest of poplars and pines from the road down to the Mississippi River. A thin yellow post in the middle of the path warned us that we were walking on top of a highly pressurized oil pipeline. Our boots crunched through fresh snow, mingling with scattered bursts of footprints that looked like tiny arrows. "Wild turkeys," said Greg. This was where the Michele had spent her summer living in an encampment of water protectors. The tents were gone, the heavy machinery was gone, the cop cars were gone. All that was left were a few bedraggled banners and the ribboned frame of a healing lodge.

Michele got involved in the struggle to stop Line 3 in 2016 because of her friend Deb, an Anishinaabe woman and member of the Fond du Lac Band of Lake Superior Chippewa. Although the Fond du Lac band and council signed an agreement with Enbridge, the Canadian company building the pipeline, Deb was one of many Fond du Lac members who opposed the project. When Deb asked Michele if she'd help organize citizens to speak against the proposed pipeline at a series of public hearings, Michele said she would.

One of the most visible leaders of the campaign to stop Line 3 was Winona LaDuke, an Anishinaabe activist, economist, and one-time vice-presidential candidate for the Green Party. One snowy day in late 2016, LaDuke spoke to a crowded community hall in Bemidji, Minnesota. She reminded her listeners how, at Standing Rock, pipeline companies, including Enbridge, had sanctioned the use of attack dogs, water cannons, rubber bullets, and armoured vehicles against Indigenous water protectors. "The heartaches they caused us, the indignities, the people who were strip-searched and put in dog kennels, Enbridge is responsible for that. We are not going to forget that," LaDuke declared. "So when they come knocking over here, we need to tell them that there are no tanks here, there are no bullets here, and there are no more pipelines coming in here!" The room erupted in applause.

Over the course of two years, three Indigenous bands, White Earth Band of Ojibwe, the Red Lake Band of Chippewa Indians, and the Mille Lacs Band of Ojibwe, along with environmental organizations, community groups, youth interveners, expert witnesses, and ordinary citizens, presented their concerns at public hearings before the Minnesota Public Utilities Commission. They testified that the pipeline would cross vulnerable wetlands, violate treaty rights, endanger wild rice — a grain that has sustained the Indigenous people in the region both physically and spiritually for thousands of years — and enable as much greenhouse gas pollution as fifty new coal mines. Despite it all, the state granted Enbridge the permits to build.

Michele was with her friend Deb in the room on June 28, 2018, when the Minnesota Public Utilities Commission voted to grant Enbridge a certificate of need and approved a route for the pipeline. When the announcement was made,

Deb started weeping. Michele remembers Deb seemed to be having trouble concentrating. Deb asked Michele what was being said. But when Michele started to describe which route the commissioners had chosen, Deb told her to stop talking. Later, Michele wanted to know why, and Deb told her: "I didn't want the ancestors to hear it." Michele was stunned. "I thought: 'Oh fuck, this is deep for her,'" she said to me.

With their legal options exhausted and pipes starting to go into the ground, LaDuke and the water protectors turned to their last resort: civil disobedience. Resistance camps sprang up in the pipeline's path across the state. Many of the water protectors who flocked to Minnesota were Indigenous organizers who had met at Standing Rock. As Enbridge crews drilled under rivers and felled trees, state police armed with batons, pepper spray, and rubber bullets cleared their path. Throughout the summer of 2021, Enbridge worked closely with Minnesota police, paying for officer training, police surveillance, meals, hotels, and specialized equipment. Nine hundred people were arrested that summer, including Winona LaDuke herself.

At the camp on the Mississippi, Michele cooked and chopped wood and carried water and participated in ceremony. Some Plowshares activists were involved, although the Plowshares movement didn't officially support the pipeline resistance. The movement remained fixated on nuclear weapons, committed to its well-worn formula of symbolic disruptions through civil disobedience and arrest. Michele had recently come to see how much those tactics relied on a certain amount of privilege. At a Catholic Worker retreat, leaders had organized a workshop on racism and white supremacy. Instead of planning a direct action of their own, as they usually did, the group had participated in one led by Black Lives Matter organizers. Some Catholic Workers had boycotted the event. They wanted to keep doing things the old way. But the younger generation of Catholic Workers was ready to follow Black and Indigenous leadership. And they were just as concerned about climate change as the previous generation had been about nuclear war.

As the pipeline construction crews drew nearer to the camp where Michele was staying, water protectors readied themselves for a showdown. At one point Enbridge workers entered the camp and attempted to start a fight. Michele tried to defuse the situation by reading aloud from a document that outlined the rights of the Anishinaabe people under the Treaty of 1855. Then Enbridge pulled one final trick. They drilled under them all: under the water protector camp, under the tents, under the healing lodge and the placid brown curve of the Mississippi River. The earth shook for three days. Lying in her tent, Michele felt the ground shudder as the machines tunnelling under her chewed through earth and rock. Her Anishinaabe friends experienced this violation of the land even more acutely than she did. "This was their relative, and they were watching her be raped," Michele said to me as we stood on the riverbank in the crook of the Mississippi's brown body, now blanketed in snow. Naked white poplar trunks creaked in the wind. I could taste the clean brightness of the winter air. The river here was narrow enough to throw a stone over, shrunken by a summer of drought. In the midst of a water shortage, Enbridge had received permission to pump nearly five billion gallons of water along the pipeline corridor.

"Christianity doesn't see that these living things are our sisters, our brothers, our aunts," Michele said. "We see all this as a resource that God gave us dominion over. To *use!*" She shook her head in disgust. "What the fuck kind of God would do that?"

I'd never met someone so devout who swore so much. A minute later she was recalling details from a psalm she'd read that morning with a group of nonagenarian nuns at the Benedictine monastery where she went each morning to pray: "Creeping things and birds that fly, cedars and trees, oceans and mist, stormy seas." The psalm had clarified something for her. "Listen," she said. "Snow, clouds, birds, these things are sacred in and of themselves, not because they were put here as resources for us to use to glorify God; they glorify God in their own right. It's not just in the Indigenous tradition, it's in *our* tradition, but we got *lied to.* We've got to take it back!"

Under our feet, oil ran. Thirty-one thousand barrels of thick black crude passed below us during the hour we spent on the riverbank, worth nearly U.S.$2.4 million on that day's market. Or, priced another way by a calculator that measured the human costs of CO_2 emissions, three human lives. Enbridge rejects such math, of course. They argue that if Line 3 had not been completed, the oil would have been transported by less efficient means, tanker trucks or trains.

But every new pipeline locks in decades of fossil fuel use to pay for sunk costs. Energy companies like Enbridge have spent millions attacking the solutions to climate change in order to protect their profits; they aren't going to be stopped by asking nicely.

On the shelves at Hildegard House I'd seen a book I recognized, *The Powers That Be* by American theologian Walter Wink. I'd read it when I was in my early twenties. The title referenced Ephesians 6:12: "For we do not wrestle against flesh and blood, but against principalities, against powers, against the rulers of the darkness of this age." Wink understood those powers not as angels and demons fighting a war over human souls somewhere above our heads but as corporations, governments, CEOs sitting around boardrooms with smartphones and PowerPoints. The powers were the institutions and structures that shaped our society. They could do good or evil; often they did both. They were the companies that knowingly dumped carcinogens into drinking water or aggressively marketed opioids they knew were destroying lives. They were the apartheid government of South Africa and the U.S.-backed Pinochet dictatorship in Chile — both of which Wink had helped communities resist. They were pipeline companies undermining a just transition to renewable energy and the police forces enabling them. The powers had to be fought with prayer, yes, but also with conscientious lawbreaking, using creative nonviolent strategies to neutralize an opponent's power. Wink's ideas intrigued me. I'd grown up with a Christianity that shunned politics; this Christianity was fiercely political. Not in the sense of flags in church or prayer in schools, but in undermining the spiritual structures that dominated and oppressed.

Growing up I'd understood spiritual and physical realities as two parallel planes. Wink introduced me to a different worldview, one common to some Indigenous religions as well as Buddhist and Christian mystics like Thich Nhat Hanh and Teilhard de Chardin. In this view, the physical and the spiritual weren't two parallel worlds but inner and outer aspects of the same reality. God permeated the universe.

Spiritual protest uses a different calculus than secular civil resistance. While both approaches share common goals — exposing injustice, mobilizing the masses, shifting political power, and altering political realities — spiritual protest seeks inner as well as outer transformation. And spiritual protest acknowledges that there are larger, unseen powers at work. "Human progress never rolls in on wheels of inevitability; it comes through the tireless efforts of men willing to be coworkers with God," Martin Luther King Jr. wrote from his jail cell in Birmingham. Phillip Berrigan believed that, in some mysterious way, pouring blood on a missile actually helped transform structures of injustice and domination. Michele told me she believed that the rosaries, the tobacco ties, and the prayer flags she carried to the Line 3 valve shut-off site and fastened to the pipes had genuine spiritual power. "All those prayers, all those things we brought there," she said, "the Spirit will carry on the hard work."

Standing there on the riverbank with Michele and Greg, I wanted their courage. I wanted the tiniest part of their faith. Was belief in a divine force naive, I wondered, or a necessary correction to ego?

"There is a divine presence that's going to intervene," Michele said, as if answering my unspoken question.

"How do you know?" I asked.

"We trust," she said. "We've got no real evidence. No real evidence that there's some God —" she stopped to laugh at the picture she was painting "— some God who comes down from a cloud and strikes your enemies down, like it says in the Psalms. It's not like that." She fell silent. I watched the wind feather the sunlit quills of brown prairie grasses poking through the snow. Her voice dropped to a more serious note. "It's hard. It's hard to hang on to that when you're hearing everything cry out 'Please stop this!' and you're looking for a way to stop it, and you're looking for that divine intervention. It's hard to see it."

I appreciated Michele's frank acknowledgement of doubt. I tried to say something, but the words got stuck in my throat. It was impossible to voice the ache of my desire to believe. But it reassured me to know that Michele struggled too. Oddly, it was her doubt even more than her belief that fed the tiny ember of my faith. Her courage was so much greater than mine, yet she experienced the same cycle of faith and doubt, hope and fear. Somehow, her second-guessing gave me strength. Her rage made me want to kneel. Her profanities made me smile.

It occurred to me that this was Spirit. This was what

Ulla had been trying to teach me to see. It wasn't something you could observe by looking directly at it. You could only perceive it at the very edge of sight, like the faintest star that brightened as you turned away.

An invisible current was flowing under the ice at our feet. A current more powerful than the oil surging through the pipeline, stronger than me or Michele or even the nuclear arsenal of the United States. There was nothing we could do to stop it or to make it flow. Our only choice was whether or not we'd step in.

Chapter 8

COLLECTED

ON THE SAME GOOD Friday in 2022 that Springs Church in Winnipeg skipped lightly over the crucifixion of Jesus in favour of a Sunday morning resurrection rock concert, a group of forty or so people walked through the puddling streets of downtown Detroit carrying a heavy wooden cross. A cold grey rain was coming down, but the pilgrims, undeterred in jackets and umbrellas, walked for two and a half hours, stopping often to set down their burden at places where Christ was being crucified.

Christ was being crucified on the concrete banks of the Detroit River. His suffering increased each time another species of bird or frog or bee fell silent. The walkers leaned their cross against a red post with the word EMERGENCY painted on it, huddled together against the wind, and read from a printed service: "In this moment, may we listen deep to the soil and the sky and the many silences between. The earth has not forgotten our agreements. May we feel its eternal longing for our reparation and return."

A few blocks farther, Christ was being crucified in Detroit's financial district. The cost of healthcare, food, and fuel was going up for the working poor while austerity policies ate away their social safety net. "Inflation is inextricably connected to wealthy elites controlling more of the market share," the marchers proclaimed, standing outside a glass-walled office tower that had housed successive banks and mortgage loan providers. "They gobble up properties to ensure that supply stays low. They deny climate change is real to keep the economy running on fossil fuels. They spin myths about government inefficiencies and the fairness of the so-called free market. These tactics drive up prices for much-needed staples."

Christ was crucified, they lamented, each time another Detroiter lost their home to foreclosure, each time the city shut off water to another household who had fallen behind on their utility bills, each time another Black person was racially profiled or brutalized by the police. The people sang: "Were you there when the rich stole from the poor?" to the tune of the African American spiritual "Were You There When They Crucified My Lord?"

Christ was being crucified under the gilt arches of a downtown cathedral where the procession stopped to denounce the rise of Christian nationalism. "When those invading the Capitol on January 6, 2021, constructed a gallows on its grounds, they reiterated a central practice of white Christian nationalism: lynching — the American version of crucifixion."

Christ was being crucified on the construction site of a

new $74 million boutique hotel with a swanky restaurant
and rooftop lounge. A man in a baseball cap leaned the
cross against the hoarding surrounding the building's steel
and concrete skeleton. Someone else rang a gong. A long-
time neighbourhood resident and a regular guest at a local
soup kitchen had remarked that the new buildings taking
over his neighbourhood were beautiful, but they had no
place for him. "With gentrification, some people just have
to go in order to make way for more desirable people," the
walkers lamented. "Some people are simply worth more."

The Good Friday procession ended where it had begun,
at St. Peter's Episcopal Church, a red brick building with
a "Not for Sale" sign fixed to its wall. The sign had been
added as a cheeky FYI to developers who kept calling with
offers to transform the 164-year-old building that currently
provides free meals, showers, and laundry to Detroit's
down-and-out into a hip new brew pub or a condominium.
One persistent real estate agent kept asking who had the
power to sell the church, until the pastor told him only
God did and put up the sign.

One could hardly find two more divergent expressions
of Christianity than Springs and St. Peter's. One church
preaches a gospel of individual liberty and financial success,
welcomes eight thousand people a week into its state-of-
the-art auditoriums, pays its star pastor a salary north of
$200,000, and has nurtured politicians who consistently
oppose climate justice measures. The other church gathers
a motley two dozen in an aging sanctuary, preaches solidarity with the poor, has a room full of emergency water for

people whose taps have been shut off, is seen as an ally by some of the state's most outspoken anti-poverty advocates, and occasionally has to bail its pastor out of jail.

St. Peter's congregation is diverse: grey-haired elders and noisy toddlers, Black and white, homeowners, precarious renters, and people who spent the night under an overpass. The church welcomes all sexualities and genders. For more than forty years, a soup kitchen has been dishing up meals in the church's basement. When a new hotel going up next door offered to pave the church's parking lot if they could use a corner of it for valet parking, St. Peter's made the hotel sign an agreement with a fifteen-page social justice addendum promising, among other things, not to use facial recognition security cameras. The wooden pews in the sanctuary can be pushed aside to make space for community theatre performances or public meetings or nonviolent direct-action trainings. But on Sunday mornings the sanctuary is a place of holy community and public imagination.

A few years ago the pastor, Denise Griebler, preached a sermon titled "St. Peter's Is Not for Sale." She spoke of the climate crisis and of the pain of recognizing "that the place where one resides and that one loves is under immediate assault." She spoke of apocalypse. "The word 'apocalypse' doesn't mean 'the end,'" she said. "It means 'to uncover' or 'to unveil what was hidden.' To experience apocalypse is to experience new sight." She spoke of the revolutionary Zapatistas of Chiapas, Mexico, who believed that "another world is possible. A world where all worlds fit." She invited her listeners to envision such a world in their neighbour-hood, a world with affordable housing for everyone, gardens, food, community, dignity, and joy.

EVERY ONCE IN A while we are given an opportunity to experience new sight. To imagine a new world where all worlds fit. To rewrite the rules. Sometimes that oppor-tunity comes in the wake of tragedy. In 1906, the worst natural disaster in U.S. history up to that point struck the City of San Francisco. A powerful earthquake toppled homes, mansions, slums, businesses, and municipal build-ings. Broken gas mains caught fire and nearly 12 square kilometres of the city burned. The disaster left three thou-sand people dead, most of the city in ruins, and half the population homeless. But years later when people spoke of the catastrophe, what they remembered most vividly was the caring community that sprang from its ruins. The novelist Jack London recalled no panicked crowds, no shouting, no chaos or hysteria. Instead he spoke of the kindness and courtesy he witnessed. Strangers distributed food and water with calm equanimity. Tent cities were constructed to house refugees, and community kitchens served hundreds. Grocers and butchers gave away food. Transactions were made without money. In the evenings people gathered around guitars and mandolins. Racial divi-sions were temporarily abandoned.

Dorothy Day lived through the catastrophe at eight years old and dedicated her life to recreating the humanity and kindness she witnessed in the earthquake's aftermath. In her autobiography, *The Long Loneliness*, she recalled those acts of hospitality and compassion as the truest enactments of Jesus's teachings she had seen.

The details above are drawn from *A Paradise Built in Hell*, a book by American journalist and historian Rebecca Solnit. In it Solnit investigates five major disasters — the San Francisco earthquake of 1906, the Halifax explosion of 1917, the Mexico City earthquake of 1985, the terrorist attacks of September 11, 2001, and Hurricane Katrina in 2005 — and the communities of mutual aid that arose after each of these catastrophes. It turns out that popular notion of chaos and savagery in the wake of a disaster is largely a fiction peddled by Hollywood and wealthy elites who fear the loss of their property, Solnit writes. In reality, most people respond to disasters with generosity, empathy, and self-sacrifice. In the aftermath of a natural or human-made disaster, most people altruistically care for strangers and loved ones alike, Solnit reports. Those who do turn violent are more often a minority who hold power and believe the public must be controlled. In their panic, these elites often cause the very violence they fear. After Hurricane Katrina, police threatened people at gunpoint, and layers of government treated many victims like criminals and refused to evacuate them from the drowned city of New Orleans. News reporters repeated hearsay about violence and rape in the streets of the majority Black city. Meanwhile citizens were sharing food, water, and clothing and using their own boats to rescue people stranded on rooftops.

The communities that spring up in the aftermath of disasters offer us a glimpse of another world. We glimpsed that world in the first frightening weeks of the COVID-19 pandemic, when mutual aid groups formed all over the world. Young people in India organized aid packages for unemployed workers. While the Hong Kong government dithered on public health measures, a citizen movement that had formed to protest government repression tracked cases, shared information on hospital wait times, distributed masks to the poor and elderly, and set up hand sanitizer stations in tenement housing. In cities across Canada and the United States, mutual aid groups delivered groceries and medication to the elderly and immunocompromised, offered childcare, helped renters organize against landlords, and provided financial and material support for sex workers, people with disabilities, migrant workers, and street vendors. It felt like a moment pregnant with hope. "You can watch neoliberalism collapsing in real time," enthused British journalist George Monbiot in the *Guardian*. "Governments whose mission was to shrink the state, to cut taxes and borrowing and dismantle public services, are discovering that the market forces they fetishised cannot defend us from this crisis...Power has migrated not just from private money to the state, but from both market and state to another place altogether: the commons. All over the world, communities have mobilised where governments have failed."

People who joined mutual aid groups during the pandemic described feeling a sense of belonging, meaning, improved social relationships, and a greater sense of control over their lives than they'd had before. Suddenly the idea of mutual aid — dismissed as outlandish when proposed by Russian anarcho-communist Peter Kropotkin in the early 1900s and dangerous when practised by the Black Panthers in the 1960s — was becoming mainstream.

CLIMATE CHANGE CAN BE seen as a slow-moving disaster or a series of compounding and overlapping disasters: droughts, hurricanes, wildfires, floods, extinctions, habitat losses. It is also a symptom of other ongoing disasters: consumer capitalism, racism, wealth accumulation, inequality, colonialism, the fossil fuel economy, and the commodification of water and land. As the climate crisis accelerates, it is increasingly becoming a crisis of inequality. Poor and racialized people are the first to suffer from natural disasters, extreme heat, pandemics, and food and water shortages, and have the least resources with which weather these storms. Governments had to respond to the pandemic because of the speed at which it moved. The relative slowness of climate change has allowed those same governments to ignore or downplay this crisis, delaying their responses and diluting their commitments. But we will need both government intervention and grassroots organizing to meet the climate disasters that are coming and the ones that are already here. We will need to prioritize the needs of the most vulnerable and fight back against the economic and political forces that will seek to hoard water, food, and wealth for the already privileged.

The injustices that come with a changing climate cannot be solved merely by small groups of citizens caring for each other. Grassroots groups can help fill the gap when there are immediate needs, and they can pressure governments to act, but they cannot replace the resources, co-ordination, and legislation provided by good governments. And disaster studies experts have noted that the spontaneous solidarity groups that spring up during crises don't always lead to greater civic engagement when the emergency subsides. Nevertheless, disasters — both climate-related and otherwise — offer us windows in which we can reimagine our society. And they remind us that the human impulse is one of collective care and redistribution, not ruthless competition, as capitalism would have us believe.

The reality TV show *Survivor*, purported to show us raw human nature: without the civilizing veneer of society, humans would quarrel, plot, and betray each other. In fact, the show had to be heavily manipulated to produce such an outcome, as Solnit points out in her book. Scarcity and insecurity were built into the game, forcing participants to compete for rewards and eliminate each other until only one winner remained. Left to their own instincts, humans are more likely to co-operate and care for each other, as a real-life example confirms. In 1965, eleven years after the publication of *The Lord of the Flies* — William Golding's widely read novel in which a group of stranded schoolboys descend into paranoia, factionalism, and murder — a boatful of schoolboys actually was shipwrecked on an island. Six teenagers from Tonga found themselves marooned in the

Pacific Ocean after their boat was carried to a remote island by a storm. But instead of quarrelling, they worked together to build a commune that included food gardens, a badminton court, chicken pens, and a fire that they kept burning for more than a year until they were rescued. When one boy broke his leg, the others splinted it up and took turns doing his work for him until he recovered. The story was never made into a TV show.

Compassion for others beyond one's kin is central to every religion that emerged during the Axial Age (800–200 BCE), writes religious historian Karen Armstrong, as seen in the many iterations of the Golden Rule. Treat others as you would be treated. Take care of the stranger. Love your neighbour as you love yourself. Jesus and his contemporary Rabbi Hillel the Elder both said this teaching summed up the whole of Jewish law. Helping those in need is one of Islam's five essential commands. Islamic, Christian, and Jewish sacred texts are rife with admonitions against oppressing the poor, lending money at exorbitant rates, or accumulating wealth at the expense of others. The Upanishads teach that your enemy is no different from you.

DISASTERS PROVIDE OPPORTUNITIES FOR citizen solidarity, but they are also exploited by corporations and governments to gain greater economic and political control. And, as journalist Naomi Klein has shown in her book *The Shock Doctrine*, corporations have realized that not only can disasters be exploited, they can be created. In the early 2000s, a human-made disaster unfolded in the City of Detroit. While those in power responded to one emergency by manufacturing a second one, citizens in the streets responded with mutual aid, collective care, and grassroots power. Members of St. Peter's Episcopal Church read their Bibles; then they picked a side.

In 2013, after decades of economic decline, corporate flight, accumulating debt, and people moving out of the downtown, Detroit filed for bankruptcy. The decision was made by the city's emergency manager, who had been appointed by the governor to deal with the crisis. As Bill Wylie-Kellermann, then the pastor of St. Peter's, put it, one man suddenly had the authority to set budgets, privatize departments, sell assets, pass ordinances, and alter the city charter. Almost every city or township with a majority Black population in Michigan was placed under emergency management; roughly half the Black population of the state lost its ability to elect its own local leaders. The city's emergency manager began an aggressive campaign of shutting off water to households that had fallen behind in their water and sewage bills, without providing adequate warning or offering payment plans. A private company was paid U.S. $5.6 million to go street to street turning off taps. At the peak of the crisis, the city was turning off water to three thousand households per week. Households were hit with years of retroactive sewage fees or were penalized because they'd inherited previous tenants' unpaid bills.

A coalition of citizens and community organizations that included a scrappy group called We the People of

Detroit began to fight back against the water shutoffs. We the People of Detroit worked with researchers to map the water shutoffs and show how they were concentrated in predominantly Black neighbourhoods, the same neighbourhoods experiencing high numbers of tax and mortgage foreclosures and school closures. St. Peter's offered We the People of Detroit office and storage space in its building and volunteered to be an emergency water station where people could pick up bottled water. Cases of donated water were soon stacked around the baptismal font and between the pews. Church members joined a campaign to publicly shame the city for withholding a human right from its poorest residents. On a sweltering day in 2014, as hundreds of people marched through the streets of Detroit demanding water justice, Wylie-Kellermann and several of his parishioners were among a group who blocked the entrance to the compound where trucks were preparing to go out to turn off people's water. The protestors prayed. They sang hymns. They passed around a chalice of holy water. For more than seven hours they stood in the way of the trucks. Eventually police arrested nine people, including Wylie-Kellermann and Marian Kramer, a civil rights activist who had participated in lunch counter sit-ins in the 1960s. The public attention around the arrests caused the city to briefly pause its shut-off campaign. The city tried to settle with the defendants out of court, but the activists refused. They asked for a jury trial, which they turned into a form of public theatre to further expose the city's injustices. At the trial, Wylie-Kellermann addressed the jury directly, calling them the "last remaining form of democracy in the city."

Water shutoffs decreased after that, and the city said it would offer a payment plan and financial help to people below the poverty line. Still, it wasn't until COVID-19 struck and the United Nations called on governments worldwide to end water cuts for the sake of public health that the City of Detroit agreed to a moratorium on water shutoffs while the pandemic lasted.

St. Peter's imagined another way of being. A tiny church in downtown Detroit envisioned a more just world and took steps to help it become a reality. They didn't lead the struggle, but they situated themselves among the people. They saw a role and stepped into it. They opened their doors. They followed the lead of the community. St. Peter's continues to rent out rooms in its parish hall at low rates to groups working for community justice: a mutual aid society born during the pandemic, a group of lawyers who provide legal support for activists, a theatre collective, an organization that trains people in nonviolent direct action. Monica Lewis-Patrick, founder of We the People of Detroit, has described St. Peter's as a model of the "beloved community."

Kateri Boucher, a twenty-seven-year-old editor, moved from Rochester, New York, to Detroit a few years ago partly because of St. Peter's reputation for peace and justice work. "I was blown away by the way this community was living out their lives and their understanding of Christianity," she told me.

This kind of solidarity doesn't happen without conscious

effort. Kateri points to the decades of work that former pastor Wylie-Kellermann and current pastor Denise Griebler (they are married to each other) have done to build relationships with other community groups. "They use religion where it can be in service of justice and activism," she said. "They wear their stoles and robes to actions and bring a spiritual presence, but very much in a role of following the community they're supporting."

"The structures of colonialism, imperialism, and capitalism have a material structure, but they also have a spiritual dimension that's invisible," Wylie-Kellerman told me. "That invisibility is part of their power." He believes liturgical practices — carrying a cross through downtown Detroit and planting it in front of a usurious bank, for instance — make those invisible forces visible. When he and others stood in front of the water shut-off trucks, they passed around a chalice full of holy water. "It reveals how the forces are commodifying and taking what's a gift to the commons and turning it into a possession," he said.

This is a role that a church can play in an era of ecological and human crises. Not seizing the spotlight but filling the gap. Getting in the way when it's needed and stepping out of the way when it's time. Imagining another world. "The kin-dom of God," one walker in the Good Friday procession called it, "where the worth, dignity, and belovedness of every person — along with our more-than-human kin — are embraced in mutuality and reciprocity."

Almost a century ago Dorothy Day and her co-conspirator, the French theologian and social activist Peter Maurin, envisioned a world dramatically different from the one they saw around them in Depression-era New York. Industrial capitalism's narrative of competition, its methods of creating and controlling wealth, and its obsession with private property and material accumulation had created a society of stark inequality. Twenty thousand people were living on the streets. They believed another world was possible, a world in which people took care of each other, and there was enough for all, and it was "easier for people to be good." Day caught a glimpse of that world in the wake of the San Francisco earthquake. All of us saw examples of it in the early days of the COVID-19 pandemic. In some ways, the utopian worlds we envision will always remain out of reach. But the worlds we imagine are the worlds we work for. As climate disasters continue to appear, so will the powers that seek to exploit them, and so will communities of kindness and resistance and mutual care. What we believe in this moment matters. As Wylie-Kellerman will tell you, religion has the power to make the invisible visible, both the powers that be and the worlds that could be.

Chapter 9

REBORN

WHERE DOES ONE GO to settle a quarrel with God?

I chose the desert. Jesus went into the desert to be tempted by the devil. In the desert, Jacob wrestled with God, Muhammad received a revelation, and a thirsty Hagar wept until an angel led her to water. In the desert you saw visions or encountered God or found your own elusive soul. I wanted all of these things. But even one would be enough, I told myself. If there was a god, surely the desert would be where she'd reveal herself.

I'd spent the past decade and a half quarrelling with a God who lived in the sky. If someone asked me about my faith, I told them what I was not: a Bible-believing Christian. The fight was getting old. I was tired of defining myself by what I'd set aside; I wanted to identify with what I embraced. "I'm ready for my relationship with the earth and with my soul and with my calling to take on words and clarity," I wrote in my journal in early 2022. I'd been exploring new ways of being spiritual. My vision of the divine had merged with the earth in ways I couldn't fully articulate. I didn't talk about my new faith much. It felt so fragile. I didn't have answers to all the moral and metaphysical questions. I wasn't wearing the armour of God but a thin, revealing habit. What if I was walking around naked, like the emperor?

I wanted some kind of assurance that I was on the right path. When I told Ulla this she laughed. "I'm not sure there's a wrong path for you to be on," she said. Still, I wanted some kind of sign. If I went out into the desert and challenged God to show up, something would have to happen.

It was December and Manitoba was covered in wind-carved snowdrifts. I googled "deserts in North America." The nearest deserts were thousands of kilometres away, in the rain-shadow of western coastal mountain ranges.

I was thinking about deserts because I'd been reading a book with an image of an orange wind-scoured rock formation on the cover. The book was *Nature and the Human Soul* by Bill Plotkin, an American psychologist and wilderness guide who had come up with a model of human spiritual development grounded in the natural world. Plotkin described a person's soul as their ultimate place in the world. You became an adult by learning your place, your unique and mystical relationship to the world around you. Most people in Western societies were stalled in adolescence, Plotkin believed. We were disconnected from the living world around us, distracted by consumerism, busy climbing the ladders of achievement and success. As a result, we were failing in our responsibilities to the earth community. Our future hinged upon whether or not we could grow up. Many non-Western cultures had nature-based rituals to initiate young people into the responsibilities of adulthood. Plotkin drew on the mythical journey envisioned by Joseph Campbell, the Earth-based spirituality of Joanna Macy and Thomas Berry, and the depth psychology of Carl Jung to create a set of ceremonies to help people do that work. His organization, the Animas Valley Institute, hosted spiritual experiences on the land led by wilderness therapists. I looked up the website. The next event was a few months away: a week-long experience culminating in a three-day fast alone in the Sonoran Desert.

Oh shit, I thought. I was going to have to do this.

But I was afraid. It wasn't the wilderness I feared. I loved wandering the boreal forest or plunging into the breathtaking grip of a cold lake or leaning against a cottonwood watching a formation of ducks fly so low along the river their wingtips swatted the water. Fasting made sense too, that age-old spiritual discipline that focused the mind and clarified the spirit and tuned the inner ear.

"It's the spiritual part that scares me," I told Ulla. "What if something actually happens?" I'd spent much of my childhood begging God to show himself to me in some undeniable way. I'd pleaded for miracles. I'd prayed to see the laws of nature shatter. I knew people who said they had seen visions or been inexplicably healed or heard God speak in an audible voice. If only I had faith the size of a mustard seed. Evidently I lacked even the tiniest grain. But I'd outgrown that phase. I'd concluded I was not the kind of person to whom miracles occurred. Electrons behaved differently when observed. When I was around, the laws of science held firm. The natural order itself was the miracle, I'd decided: torn skin stitched itself together, starlings flying wingtip to wingtip moved as though directed by a single mind.

I realized now that I was afraid of two things. Either something would happen that I couldn't explain and I'd be forced to rethink my carefully assembled explanation of the world, or nothing would happen, but I'd want it so badly I'd trick myself into believing it had. I pictured myself sitting in front of a cactus, willing it to speak.

I did more research. Others vouched for Animas Valley. Ulla had taken a workshop with the guides who would be leading the Sonoran Desert experience. They were wise, grounded, and sincere.

Still, I hesitated. One does not challenge God to a duel and then rest easy at night.

I marshalled my excuses. Did I have to go so far away? Couldn't I do this in my own bioregion, supported by my own community? Could I trust these strangers to make space for a genuine spiritual experience? What if this was just another serving of self-help salvation — ten steps to an optimized body or a tidied life or a manifested dream, served up with spiritual practices poached from other cultures?

Another question: How would I get to Arizona? I hadn't flown in six years. Eighty percent of people on the planet had never set foot on an airplane. I didn't know if I was ready to rejoin the 20 percent who were swaddling the planet in jet fuel fumes. Driving a car 6,000 kilometres was almost as bad. Train travel had the smallest carbon footprint by far, but tickets were triple the cost of a flight. Since there was no direct route from Winnipeg to Tuscon, I'd have to drive across the border into North Dakota and catch a midnight train to Chicago, where I'd connect to routes heading south through Missouri and Arkansas and west across Texas. The journey to Tuscon would take five days, the return trip even longer. Granted, it was still a lightning pace compared to the transportation methods of our low-carbon past, but I felt bad about leaving Mona with both children and a full-time job for three weeks.

I asked her what I should do.

"What do you *want* to do?" she said.

"I asked for your opinion."

"I know, but I can't be the one to tell you. You have to know."

"Fine. You're not going to help."

"Okay," she said, "I think you should go."

"Why?"

"Because." She had the look in her eye I'd come to know. "You don't need more information. You need an experience. You need to go deep inside yourself."

She was right, of course. I took a deep breath and called Amtrak to book my itinerary through eight different states. If I was going to learn my place in the universe, dammit, it would be with my feet close to the ground.

ANIMAS VALLEY ENCOURAGED EACH of us to tell some
friends or family members about our intentions for the
journey and invite them to pray or light candles for us
during the days of our solo fast. I made a list of everyone
I could think of who wouldn't be weirded out by what I was
about to do. It was a short list: one family of four with
whom we were close and Roberta, a silver-haired Buddhist,
godmother to both of our children. She'd once drawn a
portrait of me as the Green Man, the medieval forest spirit
whose face could be found carved into corbels and pillars
of ancient churches, often wreathed in leaves or sprout-
ing vines from his nostrils. Some considered him a bridge
between pagan and Christian beliefs. I asked Roberta if
she'd send me off with a ceremony. A few days before my
departure, she came over and anointed me with rosewater.
My son loved it. He rubbed my hands and feet and gave
me long tender hugs. My daughter sat on the couch reading a book, occasionally raising her eyes to glare at me and
declare, "You're not going!" I knew I would miss her more
than anyone.

My parents drove me across the border to the Amtrak
station, a rectangle of dull concrete at the edge of the snow-
scoured prairie. I'd told them I was going to a conference.
Anything spiritual that wasn't explicitly Christian made
them anxious. Inwardly, I was still having trouble explain-
ing it, even to myself. I felt fragile, nervous; I knew I couldn't
handle anyone else's doubts on top of my own. My parents
were enthusiastic about the trip. My dad insisted on paying
for the gas and the COVID-19 tests they would need to

get back into Canada. "We're proud of your writing," he said. My mom was full of questions. Why was I bringing a backpack and tent? Who were the speakers? I kept my answers vague and cheerful. When I said the "conference" involved camping in the desert my mother said, "Just like Jesus." She pointed out that Lent was about to begin, the period in the Christian calendar commemorating Jesus's forty days of fasting in the wilderness. Her words caught me off guard. I hadn't said anything to her about fasting. "Yeah," I mumbled. "Just like Jesus."

FOUR DAYS AFTER DEPARTING that frozen outpost in North Dakota, I woke on the train to the sun rising over the thirsty plains of southern Texas, wide expanses of stony soil populated by tufts of khaki grass and hunkering mesquite bushes and spiky-haired yuccas. We arrowed across the folds and gullies of a parched landscape that stunned me with its fierce, determined beauty. When a Texan on the train complained about crossing "a whole lotta nothing," I felt offended on the desert's behalf. The last evening spread its yellow glow across the grey desert, and I felt loneliness wrap itself around my throat. It was dark when I stepped off the train into the nightlife of Tuscon, but the breeze was warm and tender. Mariachi music poured from a plaza lit by strings of golden bulbs. A tanned, white-haired couple who had disembarked from a private luxury car struck up a conversation while I waited for my cab. The man wanted to know why I'd taken the train. When

I mentioned climate change, he nudged his wife. "You hear that? We got ourselves a young man from the future here! He doesn't fly because of all that yucky pollution!"

My taxi took me to the outskirts of Tuscon, where the houses petered out and the mesquite and cacti of Saguaro National Park took over. The retreat centre, a handful of brick buildings with red tile roofs, was dark when I got there. I pitched my tent by the light of my headlamp on a patch of gravel between needle-fingered entities I could hardly see but could certainly feel. I could hear coyotes yapping.

I woke the next morning to a cool blue dawn. A red snout of rock thrust upward to the west of me, lit by the rising sun. I was surrounded by a thousand thorny, unfamiliar plants. More birds were speaking at once than I'd ever heard in my life. I lay still, listening, rapt.

The rest of the participants arrived throughout the day and pitched their tents among the cacti that surrounded the retreat centre. There were thirteen of us, plus our two guides: Greg, a beekeeper with a Kentucky accent, dark mischievous eyebrows, and a Rilke poem on his tongue for every occasion; and Leah, a yogi and wilderness therapist whose face lit up with a slow, quiet smile when she listened to you speak. As we introduced ourselves around a bonfire that night, Leah spoke of "the suffering of the human and the more-than-human world" we were causing. Ecological grief was common among people who participated in Animas Valley programs, she said. Her calling, as she saw it, was to guide them toward emotional and spiritual wholeness. "If we stay on the journey long enough, we'll find the deeper layers of our own psyche, our deepest longing," she said. This longing would lead us to our roles in helping repair the world, she said. "That's the boon we can bring back to our communities."

Over the next few days Leah and Greg steered us gently out of the "day world," as they called it — the world of ego and achievement — into the night world of intuition and spirit. When we introduced ourselves, we were told to do so not with a career or livelihood but by sharing a dream, an early childhood memory, or an experience in nature. I told the story of my uncanny encounter with the poplar trees along the Manigotagan River on that autumn camping trip with my uncle and cousin, my canoe gliding on a riverpane of glass between the dark, watching trunks. Leah encouraged us to record our dreams, and every morning at breakfast we took turns recounting them while Greg and Leah asked questions to help draw out their meaning. During the day, we sat in a circle under the desert sun and shared our stories. A young, softspoken Finnish man said he was on a spiritual journey across the Americas to learn how he could participate in "the Great Turning" — as Joanna Macy put it — or, failing that, to bear witness to "the Great Unravelling." He'd grown up secular and had practised various forms of meditation as an adult. One day, on a whim, he'd asked the Holy Spirit to join him in his mediation. And then, to his surprise, he'd felt a warm presence enter the room. "I really didn't want the Christian God to get involved," he told me. "But what could I do?" He'd started wearing a wooden cross on a string around his neck. A permaculture farmer living out of his truck said he was trying to strip off the mask of toxic masculinity he'd been taught to wear as a child. A retired civil servant from Denver had been surprised to discover threads linking the earth-based spirituality he'd embraced as an adult with mystics in his own Jewish heritage. Nine of the thirteen participants were men. I couldn't remember ever sitting among a group of men who spoke so vulnerably and honestly about their emotional and spiritual selves. A young dad, bear-like with a black beard, sobbed as he talked about a traumatic separation from his ex and his quest to learn to be a better father. "When my daughter asked me why it hurt so much, I looked into her eyes and saw galaxies," he said. I could feel his sorrow and his wonder. My chest ached, remembering my own children, thousands of kilometres away. I touched him on the shoulder, and he turned around and wrapped me in a fierce hug.

Our guides sent us on regular walks into the desert with instructions to speak to other living things. "Sit in the presence of a dying cactus," Leah suggested. "Ask her what it feels like to die and to nourish other life. What if the saguaro and this mountain know more than you do? What if humans are not the smartest beings on the planet?" The goal of all this was to learn to listen to our muse, that quiet, imaginative, intuitive part of ourselves who could guide us to our true and necessary work. We were also learning practices that we could use on our solo fasts. Each day brought us closer to the time when we'd venture out into the desert alone.

"Is anyone in the wrong place?" Greg asked us all one morning. "It's not too late to change your mind. We'll honour that."

It had taken me a day or two to fully give myself over to the experience, to trust our guides. But I could see that there was nothing showy about what they were doing. They were not gurus amassing followers. They simply created the container. We — and the land — were doing the work. And I could see the fruits of that work already in the circle. I'd attended enough religious services in my life to know the difference between a spectacle designed to build an audience and a community tending to the hard work of spiritual growth. Our guides also acknowledged that Indigenous Peoples hadn't lost their spiritual relationship with the land the way Europeans had, and they made it clear we were not here to borrow or steal cultural practices without permission.

So when Greg asked us whether we were in the right place, I thought: I am exactly where I need to be. I'd been thirsting for something like this. In the world that I inhabited, climate justice work and spirituality occurred largely in separate spheres. The people who organized street protests were generally not the same ones who gathered for prayer. Among Indigenous activists I'd been with in Wet'suwet'en territory, that divide was not there; the spiritual was braided together with the political, ceremony was always present. But Indigenous spiritual traditions were not mine. I needed to find the spiritual path that was mine to follow.

When my turn to speak came, I felt tears rise in my throat. I shared my grief over the harm that humans were doing to the species and ecosystems of the planet. I spoke about collapsing insect and bird populations and the devastation caused by colonial greed. I mentioned the traumas Indigenous Peoples had endured on this land and the land where I lived. I talked about the suffering I feared for the people I loved, including my own children. "What I long for most deeply is to know my place," I said, "to know the work that is mine to do, and to trust the earth to hold me and my loved ones. To not be afraid. I need someone to help me carry all of this. Who is holding me?"

Who is holding me? I brought that question with me one night on a walk in the desert. After supper our guides sent us out to wander in the dark. I had my headlamp in my pocket in case of rattlesnakes but I didn't turn it on. I walked to where the road ended and Saguaro National Park began and picked my way along a stony path lit by the pale crescent moon. The path twisted upward between cactus-covered ridges cut out against the stars. Below me Tuscon glittered like a jewelled fruit salad held in the dark bowl of the surrounding hills. I stopped at a crest and sat on a rock with my back to the city and my face to the strange and mysterious wind that came stealing over the desert, and I asked my question: "Who is holding me?"

I didn't get an answer.

I took the question with me again when we were sent out to wander the next afternoon. This time I found myself sitting in a scrap of mesquite shade on the sandy bottom of a dry wash. It felt weird to talk to features of the landscape. Our guides encouraged us to acknowledge their living presence by speaking to them aloud. But something in me resisted. I couldn't interact with the natural world as though it were human; the living things around us deserved to be respected as non-human beings. I knew the creek bed would not answer me in words, and yet I wanted a deeper communication. "I don't know how to relate to something that's not a person," I found myself whispering through the thickness in my throat.

On the fourth day we all packed up our tents and drove out to a ranch in a canyon from where we'd be venturing out for our solos on the land. I shared a vehicle with Jon, the Jewish mystic. Listening to him talk, I found myself envying what he had: a spirituality deeply in touch with the earth that was also rooted in his own people's traditions.

We began fasting the next day after breakfast. We would fast for one day together, our guides told me, before we set off alone. That night we had a ceremony around a bonfire. Our guides invited us to each burn an item that represented something we were leaving behind. One man burned his military epaulettes with their insignia of rank. He'd decided to quit his career in the U.S. Air Force and start growing food.

I burned a tiny book I'd stitched together from scraps of leather. On the cover I'd drawn a narrow road leading to a golden cross. As I watched the book flare up in a yellow tongue, I said farewell to a form of religion that was patriarchal, colonial, supremacist, exclusivist, and anthropocentric. But I was also saying goodbye to my fight with it. I'd been resisting so hard that I'd forgotten how to listen to the mystery.

That night I woke up in my sleeping bag sweaty with fear. What if I couldn't make it through the fast? What if I got too cold, too hungry, too weak? What if I was overwhelmed by my own fears? Should I tell the guides I couldn't do it? I managed to talk myself down from the pinnacle and fell back asleep.

At dawn we readied our packs, filled our water bottles, and gathered on the dry grass in front of the ranch house. The sun rimmed the western walls of the canyon. We stood in a circle. "You are creating a portal," said Leah. "Once you step through it, we won't see you until you return." She instructed each of us to place an item on the ground that would call us back to the day world when our time in the shadow world was complete. I set down my travel mug, the twin of Mona's. Under it I slipped a piece of paper on which I'd written my question: *Who is holding me?* Leah walked around the circle whispering words from Rumi:

The breeze at dawn has secrets to tell you.
Don't go back to sleep.
You must ask for what you really want.
Don't go back to sleep.
People are going back and forth across the doorsill
Where the two worlds touch.
The door is round and open.
Don't go back to sleep.

One by one, we stepped over the doorsill.

MY CAMPSITE WAS ONLY about a fifteen-minute hike from the ranch. We'd been sent out the previous afternoon to find our solo spots. I had hiked along a clear stream lined with cottonwoods that snaked along the bottom of the canyon. I didn't want to camp by the stream. The landscape I envisioned for my fast was an ascetic one; a plain of sharp rocks and gaunt grasses, maybe a scrap of shade under a thornbush. A thirsty place. The kind of place where God might show up with a bone to pick. But each time I had tried to climb out of the canyon, its steep walls thwarted me. Rocks avalanched under my boots. I slipped and grabbed at a branch, which turned out to be the needled arm of saguaro cactus. With bloody hands, my face soaked in sweat, and my body shaky with exertion, I sat down to catch my breath and drink some water. I hadn't eaten since breakfast. I still had three more days to go. I was here to listen to the land, wasn't I? Maybe it was trying to tell me something. I realized I was sitting on a flat patch of sandy soil in the shade of a cottonwood tree, an idyllic camping spot. The message couldn't have been more clear. "Okay," I muttered. "You win this round."

This was the place I now returned to. I dropped my pack at the roots of the cottonwood, laid a hand on the tree's thick, grooved bark, and thanked it for its shelter.

When I'd paddled the Manigotagan River with my uncle, the river steward, an Indigenous man named Charlie, had told us to put down tobacco before we pitched our tents to let the spirits know we meant no harm. Otherwise we might have nightmares, he said. I wanted to do something similar here to acknowledge the Apache people who had inhabited and cared for this land for centuries and whose ancestors were buried here. Leah had told us the story of the Camp Grant Massacre, a horrific event that had occurred in this very canyon only a few kilometres to the east of where we were. On the morning of April 30, 1871, a group of white settlers, Mexican Americans, and members of a rival First Nation attacked a community of Aravaipa and Pinal Apache, whom they blamed for raids on their crops. The Apache people, displaced by settler expansion, had been fleeing the assaults of the U.S. Army and had agreed to turn in their weapons in exchange for being left alone. They had very little food and were nearing the point of starvation. Most of the men were out hunting when the vigilantes crept up to their camp and clubbed to death about 120 women and children in their sleep. Some twenty children who were among the few survivors were taken prisoner and sold into slavery in Mexico. An Apache chief named Eskiminzin, who survived the massacre, said the attackers "had acted as though they had neither heads nor hearts."

Less than an hour's drive away, descendants of these Apache were fighting to protect Oak Flat or Chi'chil Bildagoteel, a sacred piece of their homeland that a multinational mining company was seeking to destroy with a copper mine that would transform a flourishing desert ecosystem into a crater three kilometres wide.

The theft and plunder of Indigenous lands was ongoing. I wanted the Apache ancestors to know that I came with good intentions. I would take nothing that wasn't freely given. I came only to learn. I asked their forgiveness and for permission to rest gently on their land for three nights. I put down a pinch of tobacco. Sensing no disapproval, I began to set up my tent.

MY FIRST INKLING THAT my sojourn might turn out to be more difficult than I'd anticipated came almost right away. With my tent set up, I realized there was nothing more to do. No meals to prepare, nowhere to get to. The only book I had with me was a slim collection of Mary Oliver poems, aptly titled *Thirst*. Our guides had encouraged us to leave behind anything that might distract us from what the land might have to say to us. Gradually I became aware that I was not alone. I had brought with me a multitude of fears. My fears about climate chaos and drought and crop failure and vanishing species. Fears about famine and terrorism in Burkina Faso and war in Ukraine. Fears for my children. My beloved children: I missed them so much it hurt. My fears had been waiting for this moment when I would have nothing to put between myself and them. They gathered in an army at the edge of my vision. If I turned my head to the left, those on the right took a step closer. When I turned to the right, those on the left advanced. Ahead of me lay a corridor of time seventy-two hours long. Four thousand three hundred twenty minutes. I had not anticipated this. I loved the wilderness. I enjoyed being alone. But suddenly I was afraid. Not of the desert or hunger or rattlesnakes or cold, but of the legions I had brought with me.

I stood up shakily. I needed to do something.

I'd planned a few simple ceremonies for my solo, ceremonies to help me ground myself and pay attention to the land and ask the universe the questions that I'd brought with me. I hadn't expected to need the ceremonies so quickly.

"Make a place to pray," Leah had suggested. "A place where you can go to talk to the different parts of yourself when things get hard. Because things will get hard."

I began gathering round river-worn rocks and arranging them in a circle. I sat on my camp stool and tried to remember how to pray. I hadn't prayed in years, not with words anyway. But now I needed something to fill the terrifying silence.

"God," I whispered. The word sounded strange yet comforting. I'd spoken it so often as a child. It still had the power to steady me. "Mother Earth," I added. I needed to do something with my body, so I repeated the name again, and this time I pressed my hand against the sandy soil at my feet. The earth pressed back. I felt its deep, reassuring, subterranean strength. Rilke had described God as "dark, and like a web: a hundred roots, silently drinking." I remembered that image now.

Still touching the ground, I looked up at the swath of cool blue between the green leaves of the cottonwoods and the red canyon walls. "Father Sky," I added.

Then I put my hand on my heart. "Spirit inside of me."

Throughout the rest of my solo, this was how I prayed,

using the three names that came to me: Mother Earth, Father Sky, Spirit Within. Each time I felt the legions of my fears advance, I got into my prayer circle. I touched the ground, I looked to the sky, I felt my own heartbeat. I spoke aloud. "I need you. Hold me. Hold the ones I love."

At first it felt strange. But out in the desert, with no other humans around, I was not thinking about my ego or image or politics or theology. I was just trying to survive. I accepted that the being whom I addressed was real, for the simple reason that I could not survive without her. I needed her to help me fend off the fears and griefs and anxieties and responsibilities that had followed me here like a swarm of paparazzi.

Praying calmed me. Eventually I was able to exit my circle. I sat under the cottonwood and whittled a stick. I carved four faces into it, each looking in a different direction, each representing a different part of me. In the north was my nurturing adult; in the east, my innocent child; in the south, my wild Green Man; in the west, my muse, the intuitive voice that could tell me what I needed to do.

As I whittled, I greeted the creatures that showed themselves to me: a circling hawk, a woodpecker chiselling a branch overhead, a lime-green butterfly with a black ring on each wing, a family of javelina — small, bristly, cactus-munching pigs. I'd seen their trails tunnelling under desert shrubbery and heard them grunting and snuffling high on the slope above me as they made their way down to the creek. At one point, a whole family appeared on the edge of my campsite. They tested the air with their snouts and

eyed me with alert pointed faces before continuing along
their way. I watched the young ones frolicking and missed
my own children so much I could hardly breathe. The javelina must love their children too, I thought. I recalled my
son's eager hugs and tender emotions, my daughter's fierce
storms. Who would keep them safe? I needed to learn to
trust them to the divine mother, to give them over to the
care of love. I wanted to teach them about wonder. I wanted
to teach them to find their whole selves and listen to the
quiet parts. I needed to do this work for myself first. How
could I ask them to trust the mystery unless I'd learned to
do it myself? There was nothing more important in my life
right now than being with my children, and yet so often
I wasn't fully present when I was with them. I'd be cooking
a meal or listening to a podcast or trying to squeeze a few
extra words onto the page as they tried to tell me about
something that had happened at school. When I got back
home, I promised myself, I would play with them more.
I would give them my full emotional self.

At five o'clock the sun dropped down behind the red
canyon walls. As soon as it was dark, I crawled into my
tent. Relief. I'd made it through the first day. In my tent,
I set up a shrine next to my sleeping bag with photos of
Mona and our children and some items I'd brought with
me: a turquoise stone my son had bought for me after he'd
heard me comment on its beauty in a trinket shop, a furry
monkey my daughter had stuffed into my suitcase to keep
me company, a tiny figure of Mona I'd carved from a deer
antler. I lit a candle in a drinking glass and let the glow

paint their faces. I placed each of them in the hands of
the divine mother. I said each of their names and released
them into her care.

On day two, I played. I woke up that morning feeling
light and energetic. It had been forty-eight hours since I'd
eaten, but I did not feel hungry. I sat on a gravelly ledge
just above my campsite and watched the sun kiss a pinnacle of orange rock that thrust up from the western flank
of the canyon. I decided I would try to climb to a place
where I could watch the sunlight creep down the canyon
wall. I followed a javelina trail that switchbacked up the
gravelly slope. The trail led me to an arroyo, a tributary
that cut cleanly through dark-grey rock. I wondered why
I hadn't seen it earlier when I'd been trying to find a path
out of the canyon.

A few nights earlier I had dreamed I was in an apartment building with my son, trying to get him out the door
to go home. Instead of co-operating, he stripped off all his
clothes and tore up and down the building's old wooden
staircases. I pursued him with a mixture of parental shame
and fizzing frustration. When I'd told Leah the dream, she'd
suggested that I reimagine the scene from my son's point of
view. When I did, I started to laugh. He was having a whale
of a time scampering around in the nude while his father
fretted. My rambunctious son, 3,000 kilometres away, had
something to teach me. There was a wild, shameless, trick-
ster inside me too, whom I almost never listened to.

"Maybe you should try playing when you're out on the
land," said Leah. "You carry all this responsibility. Learn

to play. Take off all your clothes. Find your wild self. Your Green Man."

The sun crested the ridge, its light flooding me with warmth and energy. Why not, I thought. I undressed. I took off everything except my hiking boots. The new sun was hot against my skin. Leaving my clothing in a pile, I continued my climb. The rock walls of the arroyo canted above me, funnelling sunlight like water in a chute. I looked down at my body, golden in the light, muscle and sinew moving easily under my skin. I moved on up the gully, weaving between boulders and twists of mesquite. The air flowed around me. I was a trout, finning its way against a swift clear current. I climbed quickly, easily, relishing my body's animal skill.

Eventually the arroyo petered out and I stood on a rocky plain covered in bunched yellow grasses, solemn saguaros, and feather-fingered palo verde shrubs. I found a flat rock and lay down, stretching my body out along its cool granite body. I did not feel hungry or weak or afraid, but taut with wild energy. My body belonged to this earth. Humans and the rest of this living world were not natural enemies. We could live symbiotically if we so chose. This was something I had known in my mind, but to feel it in my flesh, in the pores of my skin, was new.

Next to me a swarm of bees thrummed around a pink blooming thornbush. I watched them, envying their single-mindedness. "In nature, everything is itself, living according to its true purpose," Leah had said. "We are the only species who can choose to prevent our own flourishing."

When I crawled into my sleeping bag at the end of the second day, I felt happy, relieved. I was on the home stretch. But I had one more ritual to perform. Each day I'd postponed it. I knew it would be hard; I knew it might rip me in half.

On day three I dallied. I played in the creek. I whittled a spoon. I put off the thing I needed to do. By noon I knew I couldn't delay any longer. The ceremony I'd planned was a simple ritual of lament to unburden myself of all the ecological griefs and existential fears that had been building in me over the past few years. As I'd been relinquishing my allegiance to an all-powerful God in the sky and learning to embrace a nurturing mother in the earth, I'd also been discovering just how vulnerable this earth mother was to human machinations. God had once held his sword over humans, now humans held their sword over god. This was a profoundly unsettling realization.

I began my ritual by placing a candle in a drinking glass at the centre of my circle. Then I piled stones around the glass. With each stone, I named a species or an ecosystem that was being destroyed. A stone for Peregrine falcons and a stone for old growth forests. A stone for the drought-diminished Assiniboine River flowing past my house and one for the fire-ravaged boreal forests where I camped and canoed. The pile grew under my hands. I began to weep. Soon my words were coming out in wracking sobs. The artesian well of my twelve-year-old self was flowing again. Stones for cities flooded by hurricanes and for islands disappearing under rising seas. Stones for people I knew in Burkina Faso suffering from famine and displacement and terrorism. Stones for the climate refugees attempting the treacherous journey across the Sahara and the Mediterranean only to be shunned by European nations and imprisoned in hellish prisons in North Africa. I placed stones for people who had died and were dying and had yet to die in climate catastrophes. Stones for my own children, for Mona, for myself. I knelt in the circle, shaking. The ocean that had been dammed up inside of me poured out with the power of a riptide. My face was drenched. Each stone was a weight I took from my shoulders and gave to the earth. "I can't," I sobbed. "I can't carry it all. I need you to take it."

I don't know how long I was in the circle. I stopped adding stones to the cairn when I could think of nothing more to grieve. Exhausted, I staggered out of the circle and lay down on the dry leaves under the cottonwood. I'd expected to feel lighter after the ceremony, but now I couldn't move. For the next few hours I experienced what I can only describe as psychic pain. Grief had entered my whole body. I lay on the earth, afraid of the hours still ahead until nightfall. At one point I decided I would get up, pack up my tent, and walk back to the ranch. I would tell the guides that I had failed. I couldn't last three days. But I told myself to hold on for ten more minutes. Then another ten after that. Eventually the shadows began to stretch across the canyon and then the sun dipped behind the cliff walls and I knew I had made it.

I got to my knees. I put a hand on the ground. I looked at

the pale sky. I touched my heart. "Thank you," I whispered. The earth was big enough to hold me and everything else.

I drank some water. I climbed the arroyo and sat on a rock and watched the moon rise. I was bruised but alive. I thought of my devoutly Christian family members and felt a strange tenderness. They too were seeking spiritual solace from the weight of living in this time. The divine mystery was near to them, just as she was near to people seeking her in other faith traditions — Hindus, Buddhists, Sufis, Sikhs, Jews, Wiccans.

When it was dark, I returned to my tent, got into my sleeping bag, and lit the candle for my children. I slipped in and out of sleep. I had taken the fly off my tent, and each time I woke I found myself washed in the white light of a waxing gibbous moon.

AT DAWN I PACKED up my camp and hiked back to the ranch. The other pilgrims were trickling in, their faces dirty, haggard, radiant. One by one we re-entered the portal and our guides embraced us.

When all thirteen of us had assembled, we sat in a circle on the grass and broke our fasts with halved avocados lightly anointed with lemon and salt. I have never put something so holy into my mouth.

After a long breakfast, savoured in many slow and meditative courses, we gathered under the cottonwoods by the stream to share our stories. "Tell us," said Greg, fixing each of us with his warm gaze. "Who went out? What happened? Who returned? What gifts do you bring back for your people? What remains in the mystery?"

I wept throughout my telling. "I went out, and I wrestled an angel," I said. "I came back believing in god. Not because a mystical being appeared to me, but because I had no choice. It was a matter of survival." I told how I had learned to pray touching the earth. I recounted the adventures of my Green Man. I described my wrenching ritual of lament.

I also recounted a dream that had come to me on my first night alone in the desert. In it, I'd been walking on a frozen river with Mona and our children when the ice under our feet had broken without warning. We'd fallen into a strong current. I'd shouted for my family to swim to shore, and all of us except my son had made it. Climbing out on the shore, I turned around and saw him still in the water. I was yelling instructions — "Keep kicking! Keep moving your legs!" — when I realized he couldn't hear me. He was under water. The water was clear as glass and he was looking at me with large blue eyes, but he was sinking. I leaped in.

I'd woken from the dream in a panic, not knowing if I'd been quick enough to save him. I felt sure something terrible had happened at home. I needed to hike out, find my phone, and call Mona. No, I said, calming myself. If anything happened, Mona would call the ranch and one of the guides would come find me. But the dream stayed with me all that day and the next. It wasn't until the last day of my fast that I'd realized what the dream was telling me: The drowning child in the dream wasn't my son; it was me. I was the one who needed to be rescued. This was what I had come into the desert to do.

When I finished speaking, Greg was wiping his eyes. "You wrestled with the angel, and the angel kicked your ass!" he said.

Leah spoke: "I honour the protector in you," she said. "That is the fierce masculine. That fear you feel for your children, for other species, for all people — that fear is love. The deep feminine of the earth has been whispering to you for a long time. 'Trust me,' she says. 'I will hold you.' She checkmated you. She gave you no choice. She said, 'Honey, I am with you. You can't do this all alone.' To pray is to trust. It feels really uncomfortable, but you are doing it. The ice that held the young boy has broken. You are saying to that innocent child within: I need you and you need me."

Chapter 10

HELD

TWO DAYS LATER I stood on a platform in Tuscon, waiting for a train, feeling like someone who had crawled from
a deep cave into bright sunlight. The light hurt my eyes.
People eddied around me lugging backpacks and wheeled
suitcases, clamouring into their phones. "Be patient with
people for the next few days," Jon had said when he'd
dropped me off at the train station and hugged me goodbye. "They haven't all been in ceremony for the past ten
days." The night before, I'd experienced a panic attack, an
overwhelm of sudden emotion. When I told Leah, she
suggested that my experience in the desert may have made
me more alert to my own emotions. This new state might
take some getting used to, she said. Now, sheltered in the
shadow of the train station's pillared portico, I tried to avoid
meeting anyone's eye. I wasn't ready to enter the day world
quite yet. A row of columns supported the roof above me
and a small brick ledge jutted from the top of each pillar.

I could see the ledges had been fixed with metal bristles to keep birds from perching there. But on every spray of spikes a tiny nest of woven twigs had been built. Brown and white birds, small as teacups — finches or sparrows, I guessed — darted in and out of the arches between their impertinent roosts. I held on to that image of persistent life as I boarded the train and found myself plunged again into the rush and hunger that animated the world I had briefly left. The woman sitting next to me complained about the smells, the noise, the lineups, the Biden government. A Texan cattle wrangler, whom I overheard describe himself — accurately, I thought — as "a fifty-seven-year-old adolescent," paced the aisle during a delay. "If anybody on here's got a tranquilizer dart, they'd be wise to use it on me right now. Because I'm starting to get rank-and-file agitated." A couple in the dining car recounted for me every train trip, every Arctic cruise, every sightseeing venture they were cramming into their retirement in one nonstop rush.

The train carried me back east over the dusty yellow scrubland of Texas and the red clay soils of Arkansas, then north through the grey suburbs of Chicago, and eventually over the wind-scoured fields of North Dakota. The winter's crust was melting into the soft black earth. I felt like dark moist soil myself, newly exposed and vulnerable.

I called Mona and told her everything. I cried. "I'm not sure if the same me is coming home," I said.

She laughed. "I think I like the new you," she said.

On the train I read a book on art and activism that I'd picked up in a community bookshop in Chicago. This surprised me. In the desert I'd found myself wondering whether I would take a step back from activism. But the book summoned me. I realized as I read it on the train that there weren't specific things I needed to stop doing, I just needed to do fewer things in total, and do them with more spiritual intent. I needed to live each moment embodying the love that I'd felt so powerfully in the desert — love for my children, love for the snuffling javelina, love for the earth and all its frenzied human inhabitants.

During the next few weeks as my eyes readjusted to the light, as I was wildly embraced by my waiting children, as I answered questions from curious friends about my journey, I tried to keep the soil soft and tillable. I accepted that I had become a person who cried more easily, that I had space in my life for fewer things, but I had more of myself to give to the things that mattered. Mona said she noticed a new lightness about me. I played more with my children. What better thing could I be doing with my life? I could not save the world. I could not even save my children. I had to leave that burden in the hands of the divine mother. Whenever I felt a shadow of sadness or fear or anxiety come over me, I crouched down and touched her.

WHEN I STARTED WRITING and researching this book, I did not expect the journey to lead me back to god. But it did. The god I returned to was not an all-powerful God with a capital "G" and his hands on the controls, but a vulnerable god who suffered with us and with every other imperilled species. In the desert in Arizona I had cried out for something, someone to hold me. The answer I heard came not from the heavens but from the ground beneath my feet. It was the voice of every living thing, including humans, with all of our courage, kindness, and love. It was the quiet voice Etty Hillesum heard as she knelt self-consciously on her bathroom floor. It was the exultant rush of the Wedzin Kwa. It was the sound of "sheer silence" that came to the Hebrew prophet Elijah after the earthquake and the fire and the rock-splitting wind. I left the desert with that sweet silence ringing in my ears.

One cool, rainy Sunday in early September, a few months after my return from Arizona, I walked two blocks from my house to church.

In my midtwenties, when the intellectual framework of my childhood faith had started to crumble, I had quit the Christian newspaper and stopped volunteering at the drop-in centre, cheerfully expecting that church would be next to go. But, to my surprise, it hadn't happened. I had started dropping in on a small Mennonite congregation that Mona attended. They gathered in a community building in downtown Winnipeg. Once an imposing brick-and-stained-glass Methodist church, the structure had burned down in a fire and had been rebuilt as a multi-use facility. One gabled bell tower still presided over the neighbourhood, but the building at its base now housed a soup kitchen, a daycare centre, a free community play room, a food pantry, and a housing co-operative for people living with HIV/AIDS. Two congregations took turns meeting in the high-ceilinged, light-filled auditorium on Sundays. I liked the symbolism of it, a magisterial edifice replaced by a collection of community groups. The Mennonite gathering felt more like a spiritual potluck than a religious assembly. Anyone could preach. A sermon might be of a litany of complaints against Christianity or meditation on the divine feminine. Song leaders changed God's pronouns to "she" or "they." Every June we marched in the Winnipeg Pride parade carrying a rainbow banner. No one had to sign their name to a creed or set of formal beliefs. I was still embarrassed to admit to my secular friends that I went to church — it didn't fit with the worldly image I was trying to cultivate — but it felt like an easy place for us to belong, a place where I could hold both the tools of spirituality and political action. Granted, it was a fairly homogenous group, mainly white middle-class homeowners who paid their taxes and voted politely for candidates who promised more bike lanes. Yes, the church remained tied to larger Christian structures that continued to harm queer people and deny the urgency of climate change and proclaim Christian supremacy. But that didn't stop this group from struggling to bend the moral arc of the universe in their own small way. Whenever someone in the congregation gave birth or experienced a life crisis, people would pass a hat for emergency expenses and show up on their doorstep with freshly baked bread and jars of soup. I knew that if our house burned down or some other calamity befell us, these people would take care of us.

During the pandemic, our church meetings switched

to Zoom or small groups that gathered in parks when the weather was warm. I'd noticed familiar faces drifting away. No doubt people had reassessed their priorities and found that church wasn't high enough on the list. But the opposite happened to me. The pandemic had confirmed for me how much I needed a flesh-and-blood community who gathered regularly, took care of each other, and responded to the needs of our neighbourhood. I needed to belong to a group guided by a collective conscience larger than my own. We didn't need to be perfect in our politics or our beliefs; no group was. We just needed to care.

This cool September Sunday would be our first official return to indoor gatherings, and I found myself walking to church with a lightness in my step. At the door, I slipped my mask over my ears and tugged on the heavy brass handle. We weren't meeting under the bell tower anymore. Before the pandemic, when our numbers had been growing, the community centre had started to feel cramped, so we'd found another space to rent just across the street in the little-used chapel of a funeral home. I didn't like the new space, a long, fusty room with narrow windows of clouded glass and orderly ranks of pews that focused our gaze on the pulpit instead of each other. It felt, well, funereal. But none of that mattered right now; all I cared about was being in a room full of familiar, breathing people.

I slipped into a pew. We sang a few hymns. Masks muffled our voices, but I could feel tears of happiness in my throat. Come what may, these people would be here for me and for the world. And I would be here for them.

One of the pastors read a list of everyone who helped make the church function: the preachers and the music leaders, the people who set out plates for potluck meals and ones who led outings with children in parks. The volunteer who drove a truckload of food to the soup kitchen across the street, and the person who co-ordinated meals for people going through tough times. Others led rituals to help us grieve and celebrate. Still others organized letter-writing campaigns to politicians and rallies on the streets. One of our pastors had joined an inter-faith committee planning a vigil in front of a bank that was financing new fossil fuel projects.

God has no hands but our hands, a sixteenth-century Spanish nun once said. Those hands were here in this room, I thought, and beyond it, in churches and mosques, synagogues and temples, covens, and feast halls. Those hands would provide mutual aid to people during heatwaves and hurricanes. They would work to protect forests and re-wild rivers and assist migrants crossing oceans, deserts, and hostile borders. They would find ways to grow food more sustainably and would link arms in front of bulldozers. They would devise rituals of recommitment and initiation for our new relationship with the earth. They were hands clasping in prayer. They were hands holding me.

Michele Naar-Obed believed there was a God who would intervene, that the actions of people of faith unleashed some kind of supernatural power. Sleydo believed that her ancestors were fighting with her. I couldn't discount their convictions. Something mysterious was at work. God had no hands but ours, yet a spiritual force sometimes seemed to give those hands the ability to do things far beyond what we believed was possible.

We didn't need one single story, one overarching religion. We needed many new stories and thousands of spiritual communities, each deeply connected to their own watershed, their own neighbourhood, their own fields, their own city, all working together on the task before us. Real change always starts at the edges of institutions and works its way inward toward the centres of power. Among religious institutions, that transformation seems to still be mostly happening at the fringes, not in grandiose temples or cathedrals but next to a threatened salmon stream on Burnaby Mountain or in a spruce forest in Wet'suwet'en territory or a house of radical hospitality in the suburbs of Duluth. The sacred storytelling of this era of ecological shift is just beginning.

I reached down between the pews and put my hand on the cold concrete floor of the church. I felt the pulse of the earth. I glanced up at the sunlight streaming through tall milky windows. I put my hand on my chest. My heartbeat was so slight, only the flutter of a bird's wing, so blessedly small in this vast breathing universe.

NOTES

Chapter 1: Lost

We need a new story: My summary of Thomas Berry's thinking is drawn primarily from two essays: "The New Story" in *The Dream of the Earth* (Berkeley, CA: Counterpoint, 1988), and "The Cosmology of Religions" in *The Sacred Universe* (New York: Columbia University Press, 2009).

Tim LaHaye and Jerry B. Jenkins capitalized on evangelical fear: Robin Globus Veldman writes about how LaHaye helped lead rally evangelicals against the evils of secular humanism in *The Gospel of Climate Skepticism* (Berkeley and Los Angeles: University of California Press, 2019), 9.

"I Wish We'd All Been Ready": Larry Norman, "I Wish We'd All Been Ready," from *Upon This Rock* (Capitol Records, 1970).

the *unrighteous* are taken: "And they knew nothing until the flood came and swept them all away, so too will be the coming of the Son of Man. Then two will be in the field; one will be taken and the other left." Matthew 24:39–40, NRSV.

One million species of animals and plants were threatened: E. S. Brondizio, J. Settele, S. Díaz, and H. T. Ngo, eds., "Global Assessment

Report on Biodiversity and Ecosystem Services of the Intergovernmental Science-Policy Platform on Biodiversity and Ecosystem Services" (IPBES Secretariat, Bonn, Germany, 2019), doi.org/10.5281/zenodo.3831673.

Jair Bolsonaro told the Indigenous peoples: "'The Amazon Is Completely Lawless': The Rainforest after Bolsonaro's First Year," *New York Times*, December 5, 2019, nytimes.com/2019/12/05/world/americas/amazon-fires-bolsonaro-photos.html.

forged ahead with his intentions to withdraw: "Trump Serves Notice to Quit Paris Climate Agreement," *New York Times*, November 4, 2019, nytimes.com/2019/11/04/climate/trump-paris-agreement-climate.html.

declared states of agricultural disaster: "12 Rural Municipalities Declare State of Agricultural Disaster due to Drought," CTV News, August 30, 2019, winnipeg.ctvnews.ca/12-rural-municipalities-declare-state-of-agricultural-disaster-due-to-drought-1.4571924.

Trudeau announced a climate emergency: "House of Commons Declares a Climate Emergency Ahead of Pipeline Decision," CBC, June 18, 2019, cbc.ca/news/politics/climate-emergency-motion-1.5179802.

autumn of deluge: "Wet Winnipeg Wades through Rainiest September in 150 Years," CBC, September 30, 2019, cbc.ca/news/canada/manitoba/september-rain-winnipeg-history-1.5303671.

Winnipeg opened its floodway: "Red River Floodway Operating in the Fall for the First Time Ever," CBC, October 9, 2019, cbc.ca/news/canada/manitoba/floodway-winnipeg-operation-1.5315232.

A freak storm dumped: "Picking Up the Pieces," *Winnipeg Free Press*, October 24, 2019, winnipegfreepress.com/arts-and-life/life/2019/10/24/picking-up-the-pieces-5.

Greta Thunberg brought her rebuke: "Climate Activist Greta Thunberg, 16, Arrives in New York after Sailing across the Atlantic," *Time*, August 28, 2019, time.com/5663534/greta-thunberg-arrives-sail-atlantic/.

twelve thousand people massed: "'Stop Denying the World Is Dying':
Thousands Gather in Winnipeg for Climate Strike," CBC, September
26, 2019, cbc.ca/news/canada/manitoba/global-climate-change-
march-1.5299013.

cut funding to environmental groups: "Manitoba Government Cuts
Some Environmental Funding amid Coronavirus," Global News,
May 7, 2020, globalnews.ca/news/6918374/manitoba-government-
cuts-some-environmental-funding-amid-coronavirus/.

sued the federal government: "Manitoba to Sue Feds over Carbon Tax:
Pallister," Global News, April 3, 2019, globalnews.ca/news/5127053/
manitoba-to-sue-feds-over-carbon-tax-pallister/.

destroyed more than half the wildlife populations: M. Grooten and
R.E.A. Almond, eds., "Living Planet Report 2018: Aiming Higher"
(WWF, Gland, Switzerland, 2018), wwf.org.uk/sites/default/files/2018-
10/wwfintl_livingplanet_full.pdf.

Chapter 2: Possessed

A book circulated among the missionaries: Paul Stoller and Cheryl
Olkes, *In Sorcery's Shadow* (Chicago: University of Chicago Press, 1987).

Even serious secular scholars of religion: Jeffrey J. Kripal, *Comparing
Religions* (Chichester, UK: Wiley Blackwell, 2014), xiii.

the speeches of Thomas Sankara: Thomas Sankara, *Thomas Sankara
Speaks: The Burkina Faso Revolution 1983–87*, trans. Samantha
Anderson (New York: Pathfinder, 1988).

memoir by Malidoma Somé: Malidoma Somé, *Of Water and the Spirit:
Ritual, Magic, and Initiation in the Life of an African Shaman* (New
York: Tarcher Putnam, 1994).

"The spirit that animates the whites": Somé, *Of Water*, 177. Quoted
with permission.

"the most remote parts of the world": José de Acosta, *Natural and Moral History of the Indies*, ed. Jane E. Mangan (Durham, NC: Duke University Press, 2002), 162–64. Quoted with permission.

Willie James Jennings shows how: Willie James Jennings, *The Christian Imagination: Theology and the Origins of Race* (New Haven, CT: Yale University Press, 2010).

Chapter 3: Embattled

Our people, evangelical Christians, had chosen this man: Seventy-seven percent of white evangelical voters voted for Trump in 2016. Pew Research Center, "An Examination of the 2016 Electorate, Based on Validated Voters," August 9, 2018, pewresearch.org/politics/2018/08/09/an-examination-of-the-2016-electorate-based-on-validated-voters/.

faithless in every sense: Donald Trump was raised in the mainline Presbyterian tradition but does not have an evangelical background. He seldom attends church, declined to name a single Bible verse when asked, and has said he does not ask God for forgiveness. Tony Schwartz, who co-wrote *The Art of the Deal* with Trump, said he never heard him use the word "God" or cite any religious beliefs. Sarah Pulliam Bailey, Julie Zauzmer Weil, and Josh Dawsey, "Trump Mocks the Faith of Others," *Washington Post*, February 14, 2020, washingtonpost.com/religion/2020/02/14/trump-mocks-faith-others-his-own-religious-practices-remain-opaque/.

Polls show that white American evangelicals: Robin Globus Veldman, *The Gospel of Climate Skepticism* (Berkeley and Los Angeles: University of California Press, 2019), 2.

a commitment to evangelical Christianity: Veldman, *Gospel*, 2.

Eight in ten white evangelicals: Pew Research Center, "White Evangelicals See Trump as Fighting for Their Beliefs, Though Many Have Mixed Feelings about His Personal Conduct," March 12, 2020, pewresearch.org/religion/2020/03/12/white-evangelicals-see-trump-as-fighting-for-their-beliefs-though-many-have-mixed-feelings-about-his-personal-conduct/.

In the darkened auditorium of a luxury hotel: C-SPAN, "Values and the Midterm Elections," September 23, 2006, c-span.org/video/?194449-1/values-midterm-elections.

a group of eighty-six progressive evangelical pastors: "Evangelical Leaders Join Global Warming Initiative," *New York Times*, February 8, 2006, nytimes.com/2006/02/08/us/evangelical-leaders-joinglobal-warming-initiative.html.

announced with full-page ads: Veldman, *Gospel*, 5.

"The green movement within evangelicalism": Robin Globus Veldman, interview with the author, December 2020.

"I started hearing about evangelical Christians": Veldman, interview.

ridiculed those who worried: Veldman, *Gospel*, 8.

"saving the planet from those trying to save the planet": David L. Bahnsen and Calvin Beisner, "Saving the Planet from Those Trying to Save the Planet," *Capital Record*, podcast, ep. 81, August 25, 2022, nationalreview.com/podcasts/capital-record/episode-81-saving-the-planet-from-those-trying-to-save-the-planet/.

Resisting the Green Dragon: You can watch the trailer at vimeo.com/ondemand/resistingthegreendragon.

It touched a chord: Veldman, *Gospel of Climate Skepticism*, chapter 4. Veldman summarizes the history of evangelical identity in greater detail.

Some three million volumes were printed: George M. Marsden, *Fundamentalism and American Culture: The Shaping of Twentieth-Century Evangelicalism* (New York: Oxford University Press, 1980), 119, books.google.ca/books?id=9swPktfLJigC&pg=PA118.

Under the pressures of modernity: Veldman, *Gospel*, 9.

a theological handbook for Christian environmentalists: Francis Schaeffer, *Pollution and the Death of Man: The Christian View of Ecology* (Wheaton, IL: Tyndale, 1970).

didn't believe the planet could survive: Michael E. Mann (@ MichaelEMann), Twitter, March 4, 2022, twitter.com/MichaelEMann/status/1235126492306108417.

"If you've ever felt like the last two years": Miracle Channel, "Leon Fontaine's Thoughts on the Freedom Convoy," Facebook, January 28, 2022, m.facebook.com/miraclechannel/videos/leon-fontaines-thoughts-on-the-freedom-convoy/296474572357751/.

fretted about climate mandates: "For Many inside the Freedom Convoy, Faith Fuels the Resistance," CBC, February 15, 2022, cbc.ca/news/canada/faith-convoy-truckers-1.6350538.

had once been a singer at Fontaine's Springs Church: "MPs Getting Ready to Hit the Hill," *Winnipeg Free Press*, December 4, 2015, winnipegfreepress.com/canada/2015/12/04/hitting-the-hill.

"We're hearing people say a bunch of crazy things": Leon Fontaine (@leonfontaine), "Live with Our News Crew in Ottawa," Instagram, January 29, 2022, instagram.com/p/CZVOorHIj_r.

ambulance was pelted with rocks: "Ambulances Pelted with Rocks during Protest; Health Workers, Patients Face Added Stress, Delays," *Ottawa Citizen*, February 1, 2022, ottawacitizen.com/news/local-news/ambulances-pelted-with-rocks-during-protest-health-workers-patients-face-added-stress-delays.

Many in the convoy had come to Ottawa: "For Many," CBC.

"I don't know where they get this thing": Fontaine, "Live."

"Evangelicals have embraced an explicitly business-oriented approach": Jim Hinch, "How the Pandemic Radicalized Evangelicals," *Los Angeles Review of Books*, August 15, 2021, lareviewofbooks.org/article/how-the-pandemic-radicalized-evangelicals/.

"You need to get back into the word of God": Leon Fontaine Official, "No Deadly Thing, Part 1," YouTube video, April 25, 2021, youtu.be/ uhl-n16NMSA.

"the deification of the American Dream": Kate Bowler, *Blessed: A History of the American Prosperity Gospel* (New York: Oxford University Press, 2013), 227. Quoted with permission..

Chapter 4: Bereft

"a multi-dimensional experience of loss and of grief": Jem Bendell described his experience of researching, writing, and publishing "Green Adaptation" in a blog post titled "After Climate Despair: One Tale of What Can Emerge," January 14, 2018, jembendell.com/2018/01/14/ after-climate-despair-one-tale-of-what-can-emerge/.

"When I say starvation": Jem Bendell, "Deep Adaptation: A Map for Navigating Climate Tragedy," July 27, 2018, lifeworth.com/ deepadaptation.pdf.

"Resilience asks us 'how do we keep what we really want to keep?'": Bendell, "Deep Adaptation."

"The Climate Change Paper So Depressing": *Vice*, February 27, 2019, vice.com/en/article/vbwpdb/the-climate-change-paper-so-depressing-its-sending-people-to-therapy.

nearly half the wild animal populations: "Humans Are Speeding Extinction and Altering the Natural World at an 'Unprecedented' Pace," *New York Times*, May 6, 2019, nytimes.com/2019/05/06/ climate/biodiversity-extinction-united-nations.html.

warned what would happen: "Why Half a Degree of Global Warming Is a Big Deal," *New York Times*, October 7, 2018, nytimes.com/ interactive/2018/10/07/climate/ipcc-report-half-degree.html.

"We are the initiates": Jem Bendell, "Deep Adaptation Q&A with

Carolyn Baker hosted by Jem Bendell," YouTube video, May 4, 2019, youtu.be/7ElvQq-kFfA.

published a critique of "Deep Adaptation": Thomas Nicholas, Galen Hall, and Colleen Schmidt, "The Faulty Science, Doomism, and Flawed Conclusions of 'Deep Adaptation,'" Open Democracy, July 14, 2020, opendemocracy.net/en/oureconomy/faulty-science-doomism-and-flawed-conclusions-deep-adaptation/.

responded with an aggrieved essay: Jem Bendell, "Responding to Green Positivity Critiques of Deep Adaptation," April 10, 2019, jembendell .com/2019/04/10/responding-to-green-positivity-critiques-of-deep-adaptation/.

"false hope" of environmentalism: "It's the End of the World as We Know It…and He Feels Fine," New York Times, April 17, 2014, nytimes .com/2014/04/20/magazine/its-the-end-of-the-world-as-we-know-it-and-he-feels-fine.html.

Jonathan Franzen added his voice: Jonathan Franzen, "What If We Stopped Pretending?" New Yorker, September 8, 2019, newyorker.com/ culture/cultural-comment/what-if-we-stopped-pretending.

"Mortal fear in every fibre": Etty Hillesum, An Interrupted Life: The Diaries of Etty Hillesum, trans. Arno Pomerans (New York: Pantheon, 1983), 47.

"Very well, this new certainty, that what they are after is our total destruction": Hillesum, Interrupted, 130.

"When I pray, I hold a silly, naive or deadly serious dialogue": Hillesum, Interrupted, 155.

"I repose in myself": Hillesum, Interrupted, 173.

"I feel safe in God's arms": Hillesum, Interrupted, 149.

"Such things are often more intimate even than sex": Hillesum, Interrupted, 50.

"the expression of the soul": Hillesum, *Interrupted*, 90.

"I know the persecution and oppression": Hillesum, *Interrupted*, 115.

"I shall allow the chain of this day to unwind link by link": Hillesum, *Interrupted*, 164.

"heavy with the fruit of stars": Hillesum, *Interrupted*, 80.

"The reality of death has become a definite part of my life": Hillesum, *Interrupted*, 131.

"If everyone bears his grief honestly": Hillesum, *Interrupted*, 81.

"Give your sorrow all the space and shelter": Hillesum, *Interrupted*, 81.

Chapter 5: Wild

"We are at a turning point in our culture": Victoria Loorz, interview with the author, July 2, 2019.

One Wild Church convenes in a beech grove: More information on the Wild Church Network can be found at wildchurchnetwork.com/.

compassion and empathy were the enduring fruits: Karen Armstrong, *Fields of Blood: Religion and the History of Violence* (New York: Knopf, 2014), 401.

"give voice to the suffering of our world": The Council of All Beings, a ritual developed by Joanna Macy, Work That Reconnects Network, September 19, 2021, workthatreconnects.org/event/council-of-all-beings/.

"a deep connection to the earth": Loorz, interview.

put the Bible on a shelf for a while: "Thomas Berry Obituary," *Guardian*, September 27, 2009, theguardian.com/world/2009/sep/27/thomas-berry-obituary.

"the most anthropocentric religion": Lynn White Jr., "The Historical Roots of Our Ecological Crisis," *Science*, March 10, 1967, science.org/doi/10.1126/science.155.3767.1203.

Recent studies showed: George C. Nche, "The Church Climate Action: Identifying the Barriers and the Bridges," *Transformation: An International Journal of Holistic Mission Studies* 37, no. 3 (2020): 222–41, journals.sagepub.com/doi/10.1177/0265378820931890.

human abuse of the earth as violence: Pope Francis, *Praise Be to You: Laudato Si': On Care for Our Common Home* (San Francisco: Ignatius Press, 2015).

Chapter 6: Kindled

A helicopter squatted: This scene was recorded in a short video documentary. UnistotenCamp, "Reconciliation Is Dead: RCMP Invade Unist'ot'en Territory," YouTube video, February 13, 2020, youtu.be/EgfVO6U5QuA.

Take a map of all Canada's tar sands: Clayton Thomas-Müller, interview with the author, November 7, 2019.

prevented or delayed an astounding 1.8 billion metric tons: Indigenous Environmental Action and Oil Change International, "Indigenous Resistance against Carbon" (Oil Change International, Washington, DC, August 2021), ienearth.org/indigenous-resistance-against-carbon/.

report that gathered case studies: ICCA Consortium, "Territories of Life: 2021 Report" (ICCA Consortium, worldwide), report.territoriesoflife.org.

a group of hereditary chiefs: I used details from Ardyth Wilson and Don Monet's coverage of the court case in *Colonialism on Trial* (Gabriola Island, BC: New Society, 1991).

"If we come into the court wearing our regalia": Wilson and Monet, *Colonialism*, 22.

"the ownership of territory is a marriage": Wilson and Monet, *Colonialism*, 22.

"a vast emptiness": Wilson and Monet, *Colonialism*, 187.

"You are trying to invade our land": UnistotenCamp, "Reconciliation."

Coastal Gaslink had allowed pollutants to flow: "Coastal GasLink Blasted Again by Province for Environmental Damage," *Tyee*, October 11, 2021, thetyee.ca/News/2021/10/11/Coastal-GasLink-Blasted-Again-Environmental-Damage/.

"We want you to come here now": Gidimt'en Access Point, "Gidimt'en Checkpoint Spokesperson Sleydo Calls for Support," YouTube video, September 25, 2021, youtu.be/-gPZEChboDE.

"Pray for us": Tara Houska ᐃᐧᐯᐧᐠ (@zhaabowekwe), Twitter, August 13, 2021, twitter.com/zhaabowekwe/status/1426240939425685511.

During the nineteenth and early twentieth centuries: The atrocities inflicted on the Wet'suwet'en that I've listed here are recorded in a textbook documenting Wet'suwet'en culture and history with accounts from Wet'suwet'en elders, edited by Melanie Morin, *Niwhts'ide'nï hibi'it'ën: The Ways of Our Ancestors: Witsuwit'en History and Culture throughout the Millennia*, 2nd ed. (Smithers, BC: School District #54 [Bulkley Valley], 2016).

a religion divorced from place: Vine Deloria Jr., *God Is Red*, 30th anniversary ed. (Wheat Ridge, CO: Fulcrum, 1973), 205.

"a time internal to the complex relationships themselves": Deloria, *God*, 93. Quoted with permission.

she told a story about a Wet'suwet'en man: Gidimt'en Access Point, "As RCMP Build Up Begins, Sleydo' Addresses Supporters," YouTube video, November 18, 2021, youtu.be/vg6aa_TVGXw.

interview with Andrew Potter: "On Decline: Nowhere to Go but

Down," CBC *Ideas*, September 29, 2021, cbc.ca/radio/ideas/why-civilization-is-in-decline-and-what-can-turn-it-around-1.6192307.

"That is when the invaders of the North American continent will finally discover": Deloria, *God*, 296. Quoted with permission.

Chapter 7: Disobedient

Six hundred twenty-eight thousand chickens have drowned: "BC Floods Displaced Nearly 15,000 People, Province Says," *Globe and Mail*, December 2, 2021, theglobeandmail.com/canada/british-columbia/article-figures-show-nearly-15000-people-in-bc-displaced-by-floods/.

I watch a video on YouTube: Four Necessity, "Entry and Banner Drop," YouTube video, February 5, 2019, youtu.be/BprgPRAm-R8.

"From the halls of power to the fortress tower": Rory Cooney, "Canticle of the Turning," GIA Publications, Inc., 1990. Used with permission.

Only a nonviolent rebellion could save us: Roger Hallam, *Common Sense for the 21st Century: Only Nonviolent Rebellion Can Now Stop Climate Breakdown and Social Collapse* (London, UK: Chelsea Green, 2019).

fed up with the egos and denialism: Matthew Taylor, "The Evolution of Extinction Rebellion," *Guardian*, August 4, 2020, theguardian.com/environment/2020/aug/04/evolution-of-extinction-rebellion-climate-emergency-protest-coronavirus-pandemic.

nonviolent uprisings achieved their goals: Erica Chenoweth, *Civil Resistance: What Everyone Needs to Know* (Oxford: Oxford University Press, 2021).

"Is it not possible to be radical without being atheistic?": Dorothy Day, "Our First Editorial," *Catholic Worker*, May 1933, 2, catholicworker.org/913-html/.

critiqued the Plowshares movements: Jonathan Matthew Smucker, *Hegemony How-To: A Roadmap for Radicals* (Chico, CA: AK Press, 2017).

"The heartaches they caused us": Winona LaDuke, *LN3: 7 Teachings of the Anishinaabe Resistance*, dir. Suez Taylor, 2020, vimeo .com/538751145.

"Creeping things and birds that fly": Psalms 148:8, NKJV.

a calculator that measured the human costs: Nicholas Stern, Joseph E. Stiglitz, and Charlotte Taylor, "The Economics of Immense Risk, Urgent Action and Radical Change: Towards New Approaches to the Economics of Climate Change," working paper no. 28472 (National Bureau of Economic Research, Cambridge, MA, February 2021), nber .org/papers/w28472.

"For we do not wrestle against flesh and blood": Ephesians 6:12, NKJV.

Wink understood those powers: Walter Wink, *The Powers That Be* (New York: Doubleday, 1998).

"Human progress never rolls in on wheels of inevitability": Martin Luther King Jr., "Letter from a Birmingham Jail," *Atlantic*, August 1963, theatlantic.com/magazine/archive/2018/02/letter-from-a-birmingham-jail/552461/.

Chapter 8: Collected

a sermon titled "St. Peter's Is Not For Sale": The text of the sermon by Denise Griebler can be found at Radical Discipleship, November 26, 2019, radicaldiscipleship.net/2019/11/26/sermon-st-peters-is-not-for-sale/.

she recalled those acts: Dorothy Day, *The Long Loneliness: The Autobiography of Dorothy Day* (San Francisco: HarperSanFrancisco, 1997), 20.

The details above are drawn from: Rebecca Solnit, *A Paradise Built in Hell: The Extraordinary Communities That Arise in Disaster* (New York: Penguin Random House, 2009).

While the Hong Kong government dithered: Dean Spade, *Mutual Aid: Building Solidarity During This Crisis and the Next* (Brooklyn, NY: Verso, 2020), 4.

"You can watch neoliberalism collapsing in real time": George Monbiot, "The Horror Films Got It Wrong: This Virus Has Turned Us into Caring Neighbours," *Guardian*, March 31, 2020, theguardian.com/commentisfree/2020/mar/31/virus-neighbours-covid-19.

People who joined mutual aid groups: Guanlan Mao, John Drury, Maria Fernandes-Jesus, and Evangelos Ntontis, "How Participation in COVID-19 Mutual Aid Groups Affects Subjective Well-Being and How Political Identity Moderates These Effects," *Analyses of Social Issues and Public Policy*, October 21, 2021, spssi.onlinelibrary.wiley.com/doi/10.1111/asap.12275.

the show had to be heavily manipulated: Solnit, *Paradise*, 93.

But instead of quarrelling, they worked together: Rutger Bregman, "The Real Lord of the Flies: What Happened When Six Boys Were Shipwrecked for 15 Months," *Guardian*, May 9, 2020, theguardian.com/books/2020/may/09/the-real-lord-of-the-flies-what-happened-when-six-boys-were-shipwrecked-for-15-months.

Compassion for others: Karen Armstrong, *A History of God: The 4,000-Year Quest of Judaism, Christianity and Islam* (New York, Ballantine, 1993), 391.

as journalist Naomi Klein has shown: Naomi Klein, *The Shock Doctrine: The Rise of Disaster Capitalism* (New York: Picador, 2007).

"last remaining form of democracy in the city": "Opening Statement: Homrich Trial," Radical Discipleship, November 24, 2015, radicaldiscipleship.net/2015/11/24/opening-statement-homrich-trial/.

"I was blown away by the way this community": Kateri Boucher, interview with the author, May 5, 2022.

"The structures of colonialism": Bill Wylie-Kellerman, interview with the author, May 22, 2022.

Chapter 9: Reborn

I'd been reading a book: Bill Plotkin, *Nature and the Human Soul* (Novato, CA: New World Library, 2008).

ultimate place in the world: Bill Plotkin, *Wild Mind: A Field Guide to the Human Psyche* (Novato, CA: New World Library, 2013), 13.

a beekeeper with a Kentucky accent: I've changed both Greg's and Leah's names, at their requests.

"The breeze at dawn has secrets": Rumi, "The Breeze at Dawn" *The Essential Rumi*, trans. Coleman Barks (San Francisco: HarperSanFrancisco, 1995). Used with permission.

On the morning of April 30, 1871: "Shadows at Dawn: A Borderlands Massacre and the Violence of History," Brown University, brown.edu/Research/Aravaipa/index.html.

"had acted as though they had neither heads nor hearts": Eskiminzin in an interview at Camp Grant Arizona, September 15, 1871, library.brown.edu/cds/repository2/repoman.php?verb=render_xslt&id=1227634538639017.xml&view=1226416901875000.xsl&colid=55.

"dark, and like a web": Rainer Maria Rilke, *Rilke's Book of Hours: Love Poems to God*, trans. Joanna Macy and Anita Barrows (New York: Riverhead Books, 1996). Quoted with permission.

FURTHER READING

Armstrong, Karen. *Fields of Blood: Religion and the History of Violence.* New York: Knopf, 2014.

Berry, Thomas. *The Dream of the Earth.* Berkeley, CA: Counterpoint, 1988.

Berry, Thomas. *The Sacred Universe: Earth, Spirituality, and Religion in the Twenty-First Century.* New York: Columbia University Press, 2009.

Chenoweth, Erica. *Civil Resistance: What Everyone Needs to Know.* Oxford: Oxford University Press, 2021.

Deloria, Vine, Jr. *God Is Red: A Native View of Religion.* Wheat Ridge, CO: Fulcrum, 1973.

Dixson-Declève, Sandrine, Owen Gaffney, Jayati Ghosh, Jørgen Randers, Johan Rockström, and Per Espen Stocknes. *Earth for All: A Survival Guide for Humanity.* Gabriola Island, BC: New Society, 2022.

Dochuk, Darren. *Anointed with Oil: How Christianity and Crude Made Modern America.* New York: Basic Books, 2019.

Gobby, Jen. *More Powerful Together: Conversations with Climate Activists and Indigenous Land Defenders.* Halifax , NS: Fernwood, 2020.

Haberman, David L., ed. *Understanding Climate Change through Religious Lifeworlds*. Bloomington: Indiana University Press, 2012.

Hillesum, Etty. *An Interrupted Life: The Diaries of Etty Hillesum*. New York: Pantheon, 1983.

Jennings, Willie James. *The Christian Imagination: Theology and the Origins of Race*. New Haven, CT: Yale University Press, 2010.

Klein, Naomi. *This Changes Everything: Capitalism vs. the Climate*. Toronto: Knopf, 2014.

Klein, Seth. *A Good War: Mobilizing Canada for the Climate Emergency*. Toronto: ECW, 2020.

Kolbert, Elizabeth. *The Sixth Extinction: An Unnatural History*. New York: Picador, 2014.

Loorz, Victoria. *Church of the Wild: How Nature Invites Us into the Sacred*. Minneapolis: Broadleaf Books, 2021.

Monet, Don, and Ardyth Wilson. *Colonialism on Trial: Indigenous Land Rights and the Gitksan-We'Suwet'En Sovereignty Case*. Gabriola Island, BC: New Society, 1991.

Plotkin, Bill. *Nature and the Human Soul*. Novato, CA: New World Library, 2008.

Pope Francis. *Praise Be to You: Laudato Si': On Care for Our Common Home*. San Francisco: Ignatius Press, 2015.

Purdy, Jedediah. *After Nature: A Politics for the Anthropocene*. Cambridge, MA: Harvard University Press, 2015.

Sharlet, Jeff. *The Family: The Secret Fundamentalism at the Heart of American Power*. New York: HarperCollins, 2008.

Smucker, Jonathan Matthew. *Hegemony How-To: A Roadmap for Radicals*. Chico, CA: AK Press, 2017.

Solnit, Rebecca. *A Paradise Built in Hell: The Extraordinary Communities That Arise in Disaster*. New York: Penguin Random House, 2009.

Somé, Malidoma. *Of Water and the Spirit: Ritual, Magic, and Initiation in the Life of an African Shaman*. New York: Tarcher Putnam, 1994.

Spade, Dean. *Mutual Aid: Building Solidarity during This Crisis (and the Next)*. London: Verso, 2020.

Stanley, Bruce. *Forest Church: A Field Guide to a Spiritual Connection with Nature*. Vestal, NY: Anamchara, 2016.

Stoll, Mark R. *Inherit the Holy Mountain: Religion and the Rise of American Environmentalism*. New York: Oxford, 2015.

Taylor, Bron. *Dark Green Religion: Nature, Spirituality and the Planetary Future*. Berkeley and Los Angeles: University of California Press, 2010.

Thomas-Müller, Clayton. *Life in the City of Dirty Water: A Memoir of Healing*. Toronto: Allen Lane, 2021.

Veldman, Robin Globus. *The Gospel of Climate Skepticism: Why Evangelical Christians Oppose Action on Climate Change*. Berkeley and Los Angeles: University of California Press, 2019.

Wallace, Mark I. *When God Was a Bird: Christianity, Animism, and the Re-Enchantment of the World*. New York: Fordham University Press, 2019.

Wallace-Wells, David. *The Uninhabitable Earth: Life after Warming*. New York: Tim Duggan Books, 2019.

Wink, Walter. *The Powers That Be: Theology for a New Millennium*. New York: Doubleday, 1998.

Wylie-Kellerman, Bill. *Where the Water Goes Around: Beloved Detroit*. Eugene, OR: Cascade, 2017.

ACKNOWLEDGEMENTS

EVERY BOOK IS A collaboration. This one could not have been written without financial, mental, emotional, and spiritual support from many people and institutions.

Thank you to the Canada Council for the Arts, the Manitoba Arts Council, and the Dave Greber Freelance Writers Awards, who provided the financial assistance that made it possible for me to research and write this book.

Thank you to Stephanie Sinclair, agent extraordinaire, who helped bring this project from an idea to a reality.

Thank you to Jonathan Malesic, in whose class on spiritual nonfiction chapters of this book were workshopped, and to *Plough Quarterly* for publishing a version of chapter 5.

Thank you, Jonathan Dyck, for providing critical feedback and cheering me along every step of the way.

Thank you, Sarah Ens and John K. Samson, who read drafts of the manuscript and offered kind advice.

Thank you to my astute editor, Shivaun Hearne, and the rest of the team at House of Anansi who guided this book with care through the publication process.

Thank you to Martha Beach for your keen attention to factual accuracy. I am responsible for any errors that remain.

Thank you to the many people who generously shared their stories with me for this book, in particular, Michele Naar-Obed and Greg Boertje-Obed, who opened their home and their hearts to me in Duluth. You inspire me with your courage.

Thank you to Karla Tait for providing feedback on my chapter on the Wet'suwet'en resistance. Thank you to Freda Huson, Brenda Michel, Dorris Rosso, Molly Wickham (Sleydo), and the Wet'suwet'en hereditary chiefs for welcoming me to your territory.

I am grateful to the many Indigenous nations and peoples on whose lands this book was researched and written and who continue to fight for the protection of the land, forests, rivers, wetlands, and other ecosystems on which we all depend:

Anishinabek
Apache
Cree
Dakota
Dene
Gitxsan
Meskwaki
Métis

Oji-Cree
Tohono O'odham
Wet'suwet'en
Yaqui

Thank you to Rachelle Friesen, who invited me to join the Community Peacemaker Teams delegation to Wet'suwet'en territory, and Steve Heinrichs, with whom I participated in some holy mischief.

Thank you to my guides and fellow pilgrims at Animas Valley for your open hearts and generous spirits.

Thank you to the courageous and creative climate activists in Winnipeg, including Manitoba Energy Justice Coalition and the youth who led the climate movement in 2019.

Thank you to Hope Mennonite Church in Winnipeg for your kindness, care, and desire for a more just world.

Thank you to Ulla for walking with me on the path.

Thank you to my parents for your deep love and for teaching me to be a spiritual person in the world.

Thank you to my beloved children, whom I admire and adore.

Thank you to Mona, my best editor, my soulmate, my love.

JOSIAH NEUFELD is an award-winning journalist who grew up as an expatriate in Burkina Faso and returned to Canada as a young adult. His essays, journalism, and short fiction have been published in the *Walrus*, *Hazlitt*, the *Globe and Mail*, *Eighteen Bridges*, the *Ottawa Citizen*, the *Vancouver Sun*, *Utne Reader*, *Prairie Fire*, and the *New Quarterly*. He lives in Winnipeg, Manitoba.